SOLI

GUATEMALA – JOURNEY INTO EVIL

SOLDIER W: SAS

GUATEMALA – JOURNEY INTO EVIL

David Monnery

First published in Great Britain 1996
22 Books, Invicta House, Sir Thomas Longley Road,
Rochester, Kent

A CIP catalogue record for this book is available from the British Library

ISBN 1 898125 48 1

10 9 8 7 6 5 4 3 2 1

Typeset by Hewer Text Composition Services, Edinburgh
Printed in Great Britain by Cox and Wyman Limited, Reading

1

Tomás Xicay reached out a hand to shake his sister by the shoulder, then hesitated for several seconds, reluctant to disturb the rare serenity of her face. In the thin wash of moonlight seeping down through the forest canopy she looked almost a child once more, and seeing her like that he felt threatened by an avalanche of memories. Emelia was now a woman of twenty-two, but she had been only eight, and he fourteen, when both had been orphaned by their mother's murder, and Tomás doubted whether he would ever shake the sense of paternal love and obligation which he still felt for his sister.

He smiled to himself and shook Emelia's shoulder. Her eyes opened at once, and her head lifted off the Spanish grammar she had been using as a pillow. The condition of the book's cover, streaked with layers of dirt and warped by damp, suggested that this was far from the first time that it had been pressed into such service.

'It's time,' he whispered.

'Right.' She pulled herself into a sitting position, conscious of the activity in the shadows around her. She felt hungry, but that was nothing unusual.

As if in response to the feeling, Tomás handed her a peanut-butter cracker. 'There's only two more left,' he said.

'I can't wait for breakfast,' she replied wryly, easing herself on to her haunches and nibbling at the cracker.

He grinned, ruffled her hair, and moved on to check out the rest of the unit. 'Ready?' he asked each *compañero* and *compañera*. Some grunted assent, some offered a nervous 'yes', some gave him only a grim smile.

Two minutes later the column of thirteen was on the move, threading its way down through the trees. Each '*compa*' concentrated on keeping the correct distance behind whomever he or she was following, short enough not to lose contact in the dark, long enough to maximize the number of survivors if the unit walked into an ambush. All around them the forest lay in virtual silence – there was no breeze to stir the branches, and most of the wildlife was holding its breath while the humans went by. Only the bats seemed indifferent to the guerrillas' passage, and every now and then Emelia could hear the dry rustle of wings or see a dark shape glide across a small patch of moonlit sky. She loved times like this, when the natural world seemed to reach out and embrace her with its wonders.

Fifty metres further down the trail, Tomás was thinking about what awaited them in the small town of Tubiala, some six kilometres and ninety minutes away. He had every confidence in the Old Man's abilities as a tactician and a strategist, but his own experience over the past five years had prepared him to expect the unexpected, which could be anything from a sprained ankle to the loss of half a unit.

The threat of sudden death was hardly inviting, but what Tomás dreaded far more was that his sister should be taken alive, and should suffer before death in the terrible way that their mother had suffered. Sometimes this fear would wake him with a dreadful start in the forest, and he would only just stop himself crying out. At such moments he would want to take Emelia back across the mountains and into Mexico, away from this land which had already brought their family such pain. But the sunrise always brought hope to set against the fear, and in any case he knew she would never agree to leave. This land was their home, to live or die for.

The unit marched on, down the long, forested slope to where the trail joined one of the many icy streams that tumbled down from the Cuchumatanes mountains. Stretches of their path were now open to the sky, but the moon had already set behind the peaks across the valley, and the darkness was deepening by the minute. For the next few hours they would be as invisible as any group of fighters could hope to be.

It was shortly after eleven when Tomás rounded a bend in the trail and saw Tubiala spread out in the valley below. There were only a handful of dim lights still burning in the small town, but the yellow glow from the illuminated military camp on the nearby rise seemed to suffuse the whole valley. He allowed the column to close up, so that each man and woman would have the chance to bring together the maps in their minds with the reality below.

After a final exchange of encouraging smiles and embraces the column moved off downhill again. The first small group to split off from the main body comprised Geraldo and Alicia, who had been entrusted with the unit's only heavy weapon, an old but still efficient Israeli mortar which had been captured from the Army a couple of years earlier. Their task was to target the military camp, but to open fire only in the event of a general alarm being raised.

The next to leave were Carlos and Fernando, whose

job was to cover the road winding west down the valley towards Champul. They were followed by Elena and Rosa, who had drawn guard duty on the road east, which joined Tubiala to the garrison town of San Juan Cotzal. That left seven *compas* for the Hotel Tezulutlán, two to cover each entrance and three to go in for Muñoz. Tomás had chosen José and Jorge to accompany him on the latter mission.

The seven waited just above the town for ten minutes, giving the road-watchers time to reach their positions, and then slipped between the first houses and on to the steep dirt track which led down towards the church. A dog barked away to their right, and another replied to the left, but there was no sign of life in the houses, and no movement on the streets.

They edged along the side of the small, whitewashed church, and Tomás gingerly edged an eye round its corner to check out the small square which lay at the heart of the town. It was empty, but beyond it, a few metres down the San Juan Cotzal road, he could see two figures sitting on either side of a kerosene lamp outside the front door of the hotel. They seemed to be playing a game of some sort.

So far, so good, Tomás told himself. If there were soldiers outside the hotel, then Muñoz was most probably inside. Tomás wondered whether it was arrogance or simple stupidity which had brought the major to the conclusion that he could leave the safety of the military camp with impunity. According to their informant, the man received almost daily deliveries of luxury items from his family in the capital, and had turned the upper floor of the town's only hotel into a sort of court-in-exile. He hardly ever set foot in the military camp, preferring to summon his subordinates to the hotel for their instructions. And only the sadistic thrill of a punitive action was capable of luring him out into either the town or the countryside which surrounded it.

Hopefully, Tomás thought, Muñoz will shortly be receiving an overdue lesson in humility. A last lesson.

He turned back to the others, gave them the hand signal for 'things as expected', and led them silently around the perimeter of the dark square. On the far side he chose Emelia and Cristobal, the unit's two best marksmen, for the task of watching the two sentries, and then led the other four through a space full of empty market stalls and down a narrow alley to the back of the Tezulutlán. There he paused, straining his ears for any unexpected sounds.

There was only silence. Tomás led the way in through the back door, and Jorge followed, with José bringing up the rear. The three men crept through the darkened kitchen, past two young boys asleep on the mats beneath the stove, and into the corridor which housed the reception desk. Light from the sentries' kerosene lamp glowed in the window beside the hotel's front door, revealing two more under-age employees curled up on the floor. As Tomás turned up the stairs he heard the two guards outside suddenly convulse with laughter at some private joke.

The carpet on the stairs was worn almost to extinction, but enough of it remained to muffle the sound of their footfalls. Tomás carefully lifted his eyes to the level of the upper floor, and found an empty corridor lit by a kerosene lamp. All he could hear was the sound of his own heart beating like a drum.

He signalled to the other two to wait, and stealthily advanced down the corridor to where the lamp was hanging from a piece of bent wire. He reached up, lifted the glass, and blew out the flame.

In the darkness he could see a faint light shining out from under one of the doors – the one which they had been told Muñoz used for a bedroom. And suddenly he could hear the sounds of sobbing coming from inside the room.

He tiptoed towards the door, gesturing to the others to follow. With his ear up against the wood he could hear a low male groaning intermingled with the sobbing. As Jorge unsheathed his machete, Tomás took his army revolver in one hand and started turning the doorknob with the other. He slowly eased the door open half an inch, and applied an eye to the room beyond.

The first thing he noticed was two wide and frightened eyes staring straight up at him. The girl was lying on the floor, half-wrapped in a blanket, but apparently naked. She made no sound, but quickly turned her head to the bed behind her, where another girl, barely into puberty, was rocking to and fro astride a naked man. She was sobbing steadily, the tears running down her half-developed breasts and on to his glistening chest, while he groaned with pleasure, eyes closed and hands tightly gripping her haunches.

As Tomás slowly pushed the door back the second girl also caught sight of him, and the motion of her body faltered, but only for a second. Two more thrusts of her small body kept Muñoz in blissful ignorance, until Tomás was over the bed and lifting her off, and then the major's eyes opened, only to find three men standing over him and Jorge's machete poised beside his erect penis.

The latter wilted, but before Muñoz could offer so much as a whimper José had stuffed a pair of convenient underpants into his mouth. Meanwhile Tomás was trying to talk to the two girls. The one who had been lying on the floor was trying to both dress and comfort the other girl, who was still sobbing with a quiet intensity which almost broke his heart. The elder girl explained that both of them came from a village down the valley which the Army had visited the previous week.

Tomás asked her if they wanted to go home or come into the mountains with the *compas*. They wanted to go home. They knew the Army would visit their village again, but they couldn't just leave their families without giving them warning. If the villagers were expecting trouble then all but the eldest could be sent into the mountains, at least for a time. Tomás didn't argue with her, but he did insist that Jorge escort them out of the hotel and through the town's backstreets to the Champul road.

Having forced a shirt over Muñoz's head, pulled a pair of trousers up his legs, and tied his hands behind his back, José was now looking around the room, an angry expression on his face. A portable television sat on a small table next to a pile of glossy American sex magazines. There were empty wine bottles everywhere, and there seemed to be enough items of food scattered across the floor to feed most mountain villages for a week.

'Ready?' Tomás asked, picking up the major's belt with its holstered handgun and fastening it around his own waist.

José nodded, and grabbed Muñoz by one of his pinioned arms. 'Any sound and your life is over,' he whispered in Spanish, and two eyes stared blankly back at him. The man was in shock, Tomás realized – he couldn't believe that this was happening to him. In a matter of minutes Muñoz's future had turned from bright to non-existent.

They walked down the stairs, the major none too steadily. The soldiers outside were still playing their game, oblivious to events within, but the sleeping staff had been awakened, by either the noise or some instinct of solidarity. They watched wide-eyed as the prisoner was led through the lobby and kitchen and out by the back door.

A few minutes more, and all the *compas* were withdrawing from their positions around the sleeping town, slipping back up the hillside towards the spot where Geraldo and Alicia waited beside the mortar. Once gathered, the unit began its return journey, moving uphill as fast as the terrain allowed, the higher reaches of the Cuchumatanes looming above them like a huge rampart beneath a swiftly clearing sky. In the middle of the column, like an animal incapable of understanding the terrible depth of its unhappiness, Major Alfonso Lujan Muñoz stumbled along, a continuous soft mewling emanating from his gagged mouth.

Five days later, Colonel Luis Serrano, Operations Director of G-2 Military Intelligence, was standing at the window of his study, staring out at the garden. It was a beautiful dry-season afternoon, with hardly a trace of smog to besmirch the clear blue sky, and for once the brilliant colours of the various flowering plants seemed to justify all his wife's battles with a never-ending series of new gardeners. She was away at the moment, visiting her sister at the Lake Atitlán villa, but their only daughter was with him, supposedly studying for upcoming examinations. From where Serrano stood, he could see her hard at work on an even tan, lying face down on a towel beside the pool, the top of her bikini untied.

Behind him, in the shadowed study, the tape continued to roll.

'Do you remember the man Miguel Ustantil, who you ordered arrested in July last year?'

'Yes.'

'Why was he arrested?'

'He was a troublemaker.'

'Can you be more specific?'

The interrogator's voice was so calm, Serrano thought, almost Buddha-like. There was no anger, or at least none on the surface. It was as if he had accepted everything on the general level, and was only now concerned with getting the details right. But was he really 'El Espíritu', 'The Ghost'?

'Did you personally supervise the flaying of his facial skin?'

'Yes.'

Why had the idiot admitted it all? Serrano asked himself. He had been over Muñoz's service record, and found nothing to indicate such a level of stupidity. He wondered what the bastards had done to turn the man to jelly and make him sound like an I-speak-your-weight machine. Whatever it was, it had left no marks on the body, and the *subversivos*' choice of dumping ground – on the steps of the Swedish Embassy – had not given Serrano's men the chance to add any.

In PR terms the whole thing had been a disaster. Copies of the tape had been delivered simultaneously to a dozen or so embassies and all the prominent human rights groups, leaving G-2 with very few options in the matter of damage limitation. Serrano's superiors had not been amused.

He found himself wondering once more if it really could be El Espíritu. The man was supposed to have died over ten years ago, though admittedly his body had never been properly identified. Even so . . . The most reliable witnesses had estimated his age at over sixty in 1980, and the average life expectancy of the most docile Indians was not much more than fifty. It was hard to believe . . .

But the tape certainly bore the man's mark. It wasn't just a catalogue of Muñoz's overzealous interrogations and punishments – in several of the incidents under discussion the man asking the questions was very careful to draw out why the Army had become involved, and exactly which interests – or, to be more precise, the interests of which landowners – they were seeking to promote.

But then again . . .

Serrano smiled to himself. The foreign press were not interested in *why* – they were too busy wallowing in hacked-off hands and breasts and gouged-out eyes. None of them got the point, which was that keeping a primitive people under control necessitated the use of primitive methods.

It was possible, of course, to go too far . . .

'Why did you take the six men back to San Benito?'

'To show the villagers of the region what lay in store for them if they made trouble.'

'You had them stripped naked, and each man was held erect while you pointed out the various wounds on their bodies – the wire burns and cigarette burns, the severed ears, the split tongues, the hands with no nails and the feet with no soles . . .'

'Yes.'

'And then?'

'They were executed.'

'How?'

'They were burnt.'

'You had your men pour gasoline over them and set fire to them?'

'Yes.'

That was Muñoz's last word on the tape, and for all Serrano knew his last on this earth. Guerrilla voices read brief extracts from the Geneva Convention and some UN-sponsored accord on human rights – the pompous bastards! – before the voice of the questioner pronounced sentence. There was an eerie gap of several seconds, and then the sound of a single gunshot. Serrano had heard the tape through twice before, and was expecting it, but the report still made him jump.

In the garden outside, his daughter had turned over, and was treating her bare breasts to the afternoon sunshine. Behind her the Indian gardener was absent-mindedly scratching his behind as he directed the hose at the scarlet bougainvillaea.

Serrano decided he needed to know more about the history of 'The Ghost'.

The following day, shortly one o'clock, Chris Martinson was sitting in Antigua's Restaurant Dona Luisa, waiting for his lunch to arrive. The place was as crowded as usual, with a clientele about equally divided between locals and gringo tourists, but Chris had managed to get the seat he wanted, on the terrace overlooking the interior courtyard. On the previous day a bird he had not recognized had paid an all-too-brief visit to the ornamental palm below, and he was hoping for a repeat performance.

He turned to one of the two newspapers he had just bought in the square, the one printed in Spanish, and started reading the lead story.

According to the Guatemalan *Daily Planet* an elaborate hoax had recently been played on those members of the international press corps who liked to defame the nation's security forces. *Subversivos* responsible for the murder of Army Major Alfonso Lujan Muñoz had fabricated a tape purporting to contain an interrogation of the young major, and a counterfeit admission of guilt in regard to certain crimes, all of which were known to have been committed by the *subversivos* themselves. Unfortunately for the perpetrators of this vicious hoax, voice identification experts had been able to establish that the speaker on the tape was not in fact Major Muñoz.

'And there goes another flying pig,' Chris murmured to himself. He reached for the *Daily News*, the English-language newspaper for tourists and Guatemala's resident British and American community, and looked for another account of the affair. He expected to find at least a different slant – the *Daily News*, for reasons which no one seemed able to fathom, was allowed a unique latitude when it came to criticizing the authorities.

Sure enough, the writer managed to pour scorn on the official version of the story without directly contradicting it. 'We can only wonder,' he wrote, 'that after forty years of incessant defeat the *subversivos* should still have the leisure time, the technology, and the system of communications necessary, to mount such an elaborate hoax.'

Chris smiled to himself, and cleared a space for the arriving chicken sandwich and papaya *licuardo*. The trouble with Guatemala was that most of the time it was hard to believe the evidence of your own ears and eyes. The accounts of atrocities committed by both sides were probably exaggerated, but he had no reason to believe that they were imaginary. And yet the country was so eye-achingly beautiful, and not just in the matter of landscape. Costa

Rica, which Chris had visited several years earlier, had beautiful countryside, but compared with Guatemala it seemed somehow bland, two-dimensional.

It was the people who made Guatemala magical, the Mayan Indians, though how they did it was hard to say. They certainly looked picturesque in their colourful traditional costumes, and their religious ceremonies seemed like a fascinating glimpse into an earlier world, but it was more than that. Something to do with the depth of their commitment to the reality of community, perhaps. An American whom Chris met had argued that Westerners here somehow just locked on to the missing piece of their own social jigsaw – a sense of belonging. Here among the Mayans, he claimed, it had somehow miraculously survived.

Chris wasn't sure he agreed, but he had yet to hear a better explanation. Every gringo he had talked to since his arrival had felt the same sense of magic. The only people who didn't, or so it seemed, were the Ladinos, the Spanish-speaking non-Indians who made up thirty per cent of the population and one hundred per cent of the ruling elite.

Certainly the family Chris was staying with as part of his language course had little good to say about the Indians or their culture. Their ambitions were all directed towards total submersion in the wonders of the West. Exciting memories of visiting the McDonald's in Guatemala City vied with distress at there not being one in Antigua.

Chris finished the milk shake and paid his bill, walked downstairs and emerged from the dark corridor into the brilliance of the sunlit street. Antigua was a beautiful town, with its grids of cobbled streets, its mostly one-storey buildings painted in a pleasing variety of pastel shades, and its myriad colonial churches and monasteries. And all of it nestling beneath the three volcanoes: the towering Agua to the south, and Acatenango and the ever-smoking Fuego, 'Fire', to the south-west.

Chris looked at his watch and found he still had fifteen minutes before his afternoon class was due to begin. The bookshop he had noticed the previous day was just across the street, and finding a convenient gap in the one-way traffic he walked over. He was examining the window display when a reflected movement caught his eye. A man had started to cross the street behind him but then apparently changed his mind. He was now standing on the opposite pavement, staring at Chris's back. Then, as if suddenly aware that Chris was watching his reflection he abruptly turned away, and stood gazing down the street.

Chris went into the shop and, after a minute or so of browsing among the natural history books, sneaked a look out of the window. The man was nowhere to be seen.

He decided he was being paranoid.

Five minutes later, walking across the main square, he stopped to tie his shoelaces and noticed the same man, some thirty metres behind him, staring vacantly into space.

Lieutenant Arturo Vincenzo ran a hand through his luxuriant black hair and scratched the back of his neck. 'So how did they manage it?' he asked his cousin. 'How did they get the body all the way from the Cuchumatanes to the front door of the Swedish Embassy without anyone seeing anything?'

Captain Jorge Alvaro shrugged and took a slug from the

bottle of Gallo beer. 'El Espíritu works in mysterious ways,' he said sardonically.

The two men were in a bar on Zona 1's Calle 14, just around the corner from the Policia Nacional building, where Vincenzo's Department of Criminal Investigation had its headquarters. Alvaro worked for G-2, and the cousins' meetings were as often dictated by mutual business as they were by familial ties. This time, though, Vincenzo was simply indulging his curiosity – the DCI had not been invited to share in the Army's latest public relations disaster.

The early evening hour ensured that the bar was almost empty, but Vincenzo kept his voice down in any case. 'He is not in our files under that name,' he said. 'But . . .'

'He is not known under any other name,' Arturo growled. 'Do you want another beer?'

'Sure.'

Alvaro lifted a bottle and raised two fingers at the boy behind the bar.

'When was he last heard of?'

'Nineteen eighty-three. Maybe. We first heard of the bastard around 1979, but by 1983 it was looking less and less likely that only one man was involved. If there was, then he must have had a fucking time machine – his name was coming up in the Atitlán area, the Cuchumatanes, even way out in the Petén, and pretty much at the same time.' He picked up the fresh bottle and poured it into the empty glass, shaking his head as he did so. 'There's no way it could have been the same man.'

'If there's one thing those Indians can do, it's walk.'

Alvaro grunted. 'They can't fly, though, can they?'

Vincenzo grinned. 'Thank Christ for that.' He took

another slug of beer. 'Weren't there any eyewitness descriptions of him or them?'

'Hundreds of them – that was the problem. Most of them were unwilling witnesses, and no doubt most of them lied with their last breath. So El Espíritu was tall, short, dark, fair, blue-eyed, black-eyed – you name it. Absolutely fucking useless. The only semi-reliable description we had came from two English soldiers.'

'What? How did that happen?'

'Remember in 1980, when that guerrilla group took over the Tikal ruins for several days?'

'Vaguely.'

'They took about twenty tourists hostage, most of them English. The whole business lasted four days, I think. The guerrilla leader . . .'

'El Espíritu.'

'So he claimed. He would only negotiate through foreign intermediaries, and, like I said, most of the tourists were English, so they sent in a couple of their soldiers from Belize, men from that group which had handled the Iranian Embassy siege in London a few months earlier . . .'

'The SAS.'

'Yeah, that was them. Anyway . . .'

'There's one of them here now,' Vincenzo interjected. 'In Antigua.'

Alvaro was surprised. 'Doing what?'

'That's what we wanted to know. He picked up a tail at the airport – the usual routine – and on his first night here he had dinner with the British Military Attaché, which isn't routine for tourists. So we kept the tail on him and had the London Embassy check him out. He's still on active service with the British Army, the SAS Regiment, but not for much longer. And he is currently on leave, improving his Spanish at one of the schools in Antigua.'

'Your people have checked that out?'

Vincenzo looked hurt. 'Of course. He's doing just what he's supposed to be doing.'

'How old is he?' Alvaro asked.

'Thirty-two.'

'Then he couldn't have been one of the men at Tikal.'

Vincenzo smiled. 'Now *that* would have been a coincidence.'

Alvaro shrugged and gulped down the rest of his beer. 'I have to get back,' he said as he got to his feet.

'I thought you were finished for the day.'

'I just remembered something.'

Alvaro walked briskly across the street to where the big Mercedes with smoked-glass windows was parked, and drove it slowly back to G-2 headquarters, his brain mulling over the idea which his cousin had unwittingly presented to him. The two English officers, whoever they were, had not only seen El Espíritu, but presumably had also heard him speak. And perhaps, in the spirit of co-operation between armed forces, one or both of the Englishmen could be persuaded to identify the voice on the tape.

Less than a mile to the north, Tomás Xicay was one of five Indians sitting in the back of an open truck, but the only one among them who was keeping an impatient watch out for their driver. Logic told him he was in no danger of apprehension – there was no Army major's body hidden in *this* truck – but he couldn't help feeling vulnerable. Beyond the cathedral, which loomed into the sky above the market, lay the city's main square and across that stood the Palacio

Nacional, which housed, among other things, the offices of the dreaded G-2.

Guatemala City was not easy on the nerves, and Tomás found himself wondering for the tenth time in as many minutes why he had chosen to stay the extra couple of days once their mission had been accomplished. To see his uncle was the obvious answer, but his uncle had hardly been at home, and his aunt had been turned into a nervous wreck by his mere presence in the house. There would be no next time, Tomás decided. Or at least not until the war was won.

It was getting dark now, and even a couple of his fellow-travellers were beginning to stir with impatience, muttering to each other in Cakchiquel. This wasn't a language Tomás was fluent in, but the gist of the conversation was clear enough – where the fuck was the driver?

Tomás rearranged his legs on the wooden floor. Judging from detritus scattered across it, the truck had arrived at the Central Market that morning loaded with squash, but now, like the many others waiting nearby, it was empty save for those taking passengers back into the Western Highlands.

On the nearest truck three Indian women were wearing the traditional skirts of San Pedro La Laguna and conversing in his native language, Tzutujil. Tomás had grown up in Santiago Atitlán, another large village on the shores of Lake Atitlán, and thought perhaps he recognized one of the women. But he made no attempt at contact – it had been almost ten years since he had lived in his home village, and he had no desire to draw attention to himself.

The driver arrived at last, wearing the smile of several beers on his face. But his driving skills seemed unimpaired, and soon the truck was threading its way out of the capital and on to the Pan-American Highway. As it climbed the first of many winding inclines the last slice of setting sun was briefly visible between distant volcanoes, and then night descended, reducing the world to those stretches of tarmac, verge and cliff face which fell within the glare of the truck's headlights.

Staring out into the darkness Tomás found himself studying a mental picture of his father.

Miguel Mendoza Xicay had been tall for an Indian, five feet nine inches by the American count, and he had worn his hair long, the way he believed their Mayan ancestors had always done. He had not been an educated man – how could he with no school in the village of his childhood? – and it seemed likely that he had been too good-hearted to understand the realities of life in Guatemala. The family had access to a little land on the slopes of the volcano behind the village, and they had grown beans, coffee, corn and various fruits. The prices they received were always derisory, and no money could ever be saved, but the family only rarely went hungry, and there was usually the additional cash the children earned from making and selling handicrafts to help them through the worst times.

Then the Army had come, and established a camp only a couple of kilometres outside the town. The amount of land available to the townspeople shrank as Indian deeds went mysteriously missing and other claimants appeared with deeds which the local Spanish-speaking authorities fell over themselves to approve. The local people protested and the most vocal swiftly disappeared, never to be seen again, either dead or alive. Rumour had it that most of them had been thrown from helicopters, still conscious, into the smoking maw of San Pedro.

Through all these troubles Miguel Xicay had tenaciously clung to the hope that somehow the Army's behaviour was an aberration, that if the authorities only knew what was really happening then they would step in and put a stop to it. No one expected life to be fair, and no one expected the rich Landinos to behave like true Christians, but he found it hard to believe that such a campaign of brutality and murder could be sponsored by a government.

It was no accident that the man whom Tomás's father most admired was the local priest, an American named Stanley Rother. The father had arrived in Santiago Atitlán in the mid-sixties, and like Miguel Xicay he had watched the escalating brutality with a mixture of horror and disbelief. When the Army called a meeting of all the village leaders he had listened with mounting rage as the local commander blamed all the killings, the rapes, the tortured corpses, on the communist *subversivos*, and furthermore demanded that the villagers report any suspicious behaviour to the Army.

He had got slowly to his feet, and in a silence pregnant with dread, told the Army commander that no one was fooled, that everyone knew it was the soldiers who raped and killed and tortured, and that they must stop these acts against man and God.

The next morning Stanley Rother had been shredded by automatic gunfire in the doorway of his church.

Tomás's father had gone out that evening to talk with his friends, and had never been seen alive again. His body had been found on the volcano slopes a week later, minus tongue, eyes and hands. The twelve-year-old Tomás had not been meant to see it, but he had, and he was not sorry. He had needed to imprint it on his brain like a scar, because only then could he be sure never to forget.

And nor would he, he thought, as the truck laboured its way up another slope. Not that he needed that one dreadful memory any more. In the thirteen years which had passed since that day he had lost a mother, two brothers, many friends – and all of them still lived inside him.

His father especially so.

I knew him and still he is there in me . . .

Tomás's hand moved involuntarily towards the pocket where he kept the dog-eared copy of Neruda's poem. It was too dark to read, but that didn't matter – he knew all the pages, all the lines, off by heart.

'*I, who knew him, saw him go down*,' the inner voice recited. '*Till he existed only in what he was leaving – streets he could scarcely be aware of, houses he never would inhabit. I come back to see him and every day I wait . . .*'

2

Luis Serrano leaned back in his leather swivel chair, fingers intertwined behind his head, and ran his tongue along his upper lip, tasting the trace of brandy which still clung to his moustache. Through two walls he could hear the TV football match his son and friends were watching, and the faint rat-a-tat of fireworks in the distant Plaza Mayor was audible above that. Presumably the Indians were dragging one of their Jesus statues around the square, choking themselves on incense as they went.

Serrano leaned forward once more, and absent-mindedly tapped the report with his right index finger. He now felt reasonably certain that the El Espíritu who had been such an irritant in the early eighties, and the *subversivo* on the tape from Quiche, were one and the same man.

It was not a good time for his reappearance. The Americans wanted a negotiated settlement with the *subversivos*, and the Government's ability to impose one that was lacking in any specific commitments – one that avoided any discussion at all of the land issue – rested on the Army keeping a strong upper hand in the rural areas. The last thing anyone needed was the public resurrection of some old Indian hero, and more humiliations like the Muñoz business.

Serrano reached for his Zippo lighter – a gift from a former American military attaché – and the packet of Marlboro Lights. Alvaro's idea of asking the English soldier to identify the voice was a good one, as far as it went. The previous day he had read through the records of the business in Tikal fifteen years before, and there was no doubt that both of the Englishmen had enjoyed several face-to-face conversations with the leader of the terrorists. If anyone could definitively identify the bastard, then they could.

He had ordered G-2's man in the London embassy to run a check on the pair of them. The older one – James Docherty – had retired from the Army, and was apparently no longer living in England, but his younger companion was still on active service. It had taken some time, and not a little money – always assuming the agent's expenses sheet could be believed – to ascertain that Darren Wilkinson was still serving in 22 SAS Regiment. His current rank was sergeant, he was attached to the Regiment's Training Wing, and he was stationed at the Stirling Lines barracks near Hereford, some 120 miles west of London.

Serrano watched the smoke from his cigarette curl away, remembering the woman in London on his second and last visit. She had been one of the English secretaries at the embassy, with bright-red hair and pale skin. So exotic. So aggressive in bed.

He sighed and forced his mind back to the matter in hand. Mention of the Training Wing reminded him of something . . . ah yes, that business in Colombia which the SAS had been involved in a few years earlier. He had heard about it from the American Military Attaché at an embassy party. The Colombian Government, busy setting up an anti-narcotics unit, had asked the British Government to send them a couple of advisers. When one of the advisers and a local politician had been kidnapped by drug barons half an army of SAS soldiers had dropped out of the sky to rescue them. Or so the story went.

It didn't really matter how true the last part was, Serrano thought. The point was that Britain had been prepared to send advisers to Colombia to help in the fight against drug trafficking. Might they not be equally willing to send one man to help in the fight against the *subversivos*?

This man Wilkinson could take part as an observer in the sweep which was planned for the following week. And when they captured or killed this El Espíritu then the Englishman would be on the spot to identify the miserable little shit.

And he would also, Serrano realized with satisfaction, be a neutral witness to the old boy's death. No one would believe an Army report that El Espíritu had been killed, but an Englishman . . . His testimony could lay this particular 'ghost' once and for all, and prevent a host of other claimants to the name springing up in the dead man's place.

Yes, Serrano thought. He liked it. He liked it a lot.

Would the British agree? They still had a reliable enough government from all reports, though maybe not quite so reliable as in the woman Thatcher's time. In any event the SAS was unlikely to be a haven for communist sympathizers.

But Serrano had to admit that Guatemala's reputation in the world had suffered in recent years. All those little creeps from Amnesty International and Americas Watch, living their safe little lives in the rich man's world and bleating on about human rights abuses everywhere else.

How could he sugar the pill? What could Guatemala offer the British?

Another Belize treaty? The last president to sign one had almost been tried on treason charges, and the idea of sticking his neck out that far was not particularly appealing. It would be better, he decided, to go through the Americans. They had a keener appreciation of what was really at stake in Central America, and they could hardly refuse to help when their own beloved peace negotiations were on the line. 'We are so close to a breakthrough,' Serrano murmured out loud in rehearsal, 'and this one terrorist could undermine everything we have all worked for.'

It sounded convincing enough for the US State Department. The Americans could then bribe or threaten the British, whichever they deemed more appropriate. Serrano picked up the phone to call the Foreign Ministry, trying in vain to remember the name of the current Foreign Minister.

The request for diplomatic assistance was delivered to the State Department by Guatemala's Washington ambassador early the following afternoon. After receiving his visitor, Sam Udovich, Acting Head of the Central America desk, stared out at the falling snow and slowly consumed a strawberry cheese croissant before reaching for the internal phone.

'Clemens,' a voice answered.

'Brent, hi. The Guatemalan Ambassador's just been darkening my office door.'

'And what do the death squads want today?'

Udovich told him.

Clemens listened in silence, and then laughed. 'They want some Brit soldier to look over a line-up of corpses and pick out the guilty man?' he asked incredulously.

'That's one way of putting it,' Udovich agreed. 'It *is* in our interests that they get this guy.'

'That's what Ollie North said.'

'He was right,' Udovich said drily.

Clemens sighed audibly.

'Look,' Udovich went on patiently, 'I'd take it as a personal favour if you could get the Brits to get with the programme on this one.' And if you can, went the first unspoken message, then I owe you one. And if you can't or won't, went the second, then don't come to me for a favour anytime soon.

'I'll ask them,' Clemens said.

'Just so long as you don't leave them in any doubt about how important we think this is.'

'How important *you* think this is.'

Udovich snorted. 'It's not going to cost the Brits any money, for Christ's sake. And that's all they seem to care about these days.'

'I'll ask them,' Clemens repeated. 'If that's all . . .'

'One more thing. I think their intelligence boys should run a check on this guy Wilkinson, just in case. The Guatemalans want someone they can rely on – you understand me?'

'Yeah,' Clemens said. 'I get the message.'

'And they want him vetted?' the Prime Minister asked rhetorically. He shook his head, looking saddened by the impertinence of the American request.

'Just informally,' Martin Clarke said assuagingly. He was the junior minister at the Foreign Office responsible for formulating a reply to Washington's request.

The Prime Minister shook his head again, and then squeezed the bridge of his nose between thumb and forefinger, as if the shaking had given him a headache. He blinked and looked round the table. 'Any comments?' he asked.

For a moment no one seemed to have any.

'What's the current state of play in Guatemala?' asked the young man with the flashy tie who was representing MI5.

'Business as usual,' Clarke answered drily.

'Not quite,' the silver-haired man from MI6 disagreed. 'The Government claims to have won the war against the guerrillas, but the fact that they're willing to negotiate a settlement suggests a rather different story.'

'The negotiations are just a sop to the Americans,' Clarke insisted.

'That's not what our people think,' said the MI6 man. 'They reckon the number of guerrillas in the mountains is at least holding steady, and may even be growing.'

'Does it matter?' asked Bill Warren, the Junior Defence Minister. 'We're only being asked for one adviser for a couple of weeks. I'm more interested in what sort of favour we can expect in return.'

'Such as?' the Prime Minister asked. 'I don't think we'll get any better guarantees on Belize. No, I think we'd be better off treating this as nothing more than a favour to Washington.' He paused for a moment and looked up, as if seeking divine guidance. 'But the further we can distance the Government from the whole business, the better I'll like it,' he added. 'If this SAS soldier gets caught up in some ghastly atrocity then all the human rights people will be screaming blue murder at me. I think this should be a strictly military affair – a matter of shared courtesy between armed forces. With a high security rating. "Need to know" only.'

He turned to the two junior ministers. 'Bill, you liaise

with Five in making sure Sergeant Wilkinson has a clean bill of health. Martin, you get in touch with the SAS CO and tell him what's required. And let the Americans know we'll be happy to oblige them.'

The PM took the bridge of his nose in the familiar pincer grip and blinked twice. 'Now let's get on to something important.'

Lieutenant-Colonel Barney Davies, the Commanding Officer of 22 SAS, had just re-entered his office, having returned for the *Daily Mirror* he had left behind, when the phone rang. He stared at it in exasperation for several seconds, and then reluctantly picked it up. 'Davies,' he said, more mildly than he felt. He had an important evening ahead, and hoped to God this call was not going to foul it up.

'Good evening, Lieutenant-Colonel,' a familiar voice said. 'My name's Martin Clarke. Foreign Office. I don't believe we've met.'

'No, I don't think so,' Davies said warily. He'd seen the bastard on TV enough times. In fact the Junior Minister had been on *Question Time* only the previous week, wearing a striped shirt so loud that it seemed to affect the broadcast signal.

'We've had a request from the Americans,' Clarke began, and went on to outline exactly who and what had been asked for.

Barney Davies listened patiently, liking the whole business less with each passing sentence. It wasn't immediately apparent from Clarke's spiel, however, whether Whitehall was asking or telling the SAS to co-operate. 'So, you'd like me to ask Sergeant Wilkinson if he's willing to go?' Davies suggested optimistically.

Clarke picked up on the tone, and made good the omission. 'Sergeant Wilkinson is a serving NCO in Her Majesty's Armed Forces. It has been decided that he should serve his country accordingly in this particular matter. As his Commanding Officer, you are naturally being notified. If you wish, I can get you written orders from the Ministry of Defence . . .'

'That will not be necessary. I will notify him, and see to the appropriate briefing . . .'

'Good. I'll see that everything we have is on your fax tomorrow morning. Wilkinson is booked on the 10 a.m. flight to Miami this Sunday,' he added, 'connecting with Guatemala City that afternoon.'

'That's . . .' Davies started to say, but Clarke had hung up. The SAS CO stood for a moment holding the dead receiver, then slammed it down with what he considered appropriate violence. Then he sat seething in his chair for several moments, staring out through the office window.

Across the frosty parade ground the last of the sunlight was silhouetting the distant peaks of the Black Mountains.

'Bastard politicians,' he eventually murmured, and picked up the phone again.

Having ascertained from the Duty Officer that 'Razor' Wilkinson was on twenty-four hours' leave, the CO left the room for the second time in fifteen minutes, wishing that he hadn't answered Clarke's call. The American request wouldn't have gone away, but at least he and Razor would have had one more evening in blissful ignorance of its existence. Though come to think of it, the bastard would probably have called him at home.

Davies climbed into his BMW, turned on the ignition and

pressed in the cassette. Billie Holiday's voice filled the car with its smoky sadness.

He drove out through the sentry post and started working his way through the rush-hour traffic towards his cottage on Hereford's western outskirts. 'Look on the bright side,' he told himself. A couple of years ago he would have felt much less happy about sending Wilkinson into a situation like this one. The man had always been a fine soldier, as sharp as he was brave, but until recently his leadership potential had been undermined by a stubborn refusal to grow up emotionally. Bosnia – and the wife he had found there – had seen him come of age, and Razor now seemed as complete a soldier as the SAS had to offer.

So why, Davies asked himself bitterly, put him at risk for a bunch of psychotic generals? What possible British interest could be served by identifying a guerrilla leader for people whose only claim to fame was that they had invented the death squad?

In fact, the more he thought about it the angrier Davies became. A mission like this should be offered to someone, not simply ordered. This guerrilla leader posed no more threat to the integrity of the United Kingdom than Eric Cantona, and probably considerably less. And though Davies didn't know much about Guatemala, he was willing to bet that anyone faced with choosing between Army and guerrillas on moral grounds wouldn't have an easy time of it.

He gripped the wheel a little tighter, and wondered, for only about the third time in a military career which spanned nearly thirty years, whether he should refuse a direct order. It would make no difference to Razor – he would simply receive the order from someone else – but the gesture might be worthwhile. After all, he only had another three months in the CO's chair – what could they do to him?

Davies sighed. Who was he kidding? They could make his life hell, and just when he was happier than he had been for years. All the cushy jobs and consultancies which a retired lieutenant-colonel could expect to be offered would just melt away. All he would ever hear would be the sound of doors closing in his face.

He turned off the main road and thought about Jean. Did he have the right to risk whatever future they might have together by making grand gestures?

She would expect nothing less of him, he decided.

But there was also Razor's future to consider. He had almost ten years to go before retirement from active service at forty-five, and a refusal to accept this mission – always assuming the bastards didn't go for a court martial – would certainly stop the lad's career in its tracks.

Davies felt his temper rising again. The man was a national hero, for God's sake, whether the nation knew it or not. He had been one of eight SAS men landed on the Argentine mainland during the Falklands War, and one of six who had returned alive. Between them the two four-man patrols had provided early warning of enemy air attacks which could otherwise have wrecked the San Carlos landings, and destroyed three Exocet missiles which might well have claimed three British ships and God knows how many lives.

There had never been any public recognition of their contribution, and now it seemed to Davies as if insult was being added to injury.

He guided the car down the swampy lane to his cottage.

Once inside, he poured himself a generous malt whisky, put on Miles's *Porgy and Bess* with the volume turned down low, and looked up Razor's home number in his book.

It was Mrs Wilkinson who answered. Davies had first met Hajrija on the occasion of her arrival in Britain two years earlier, when she was accompanying an SAS team returning from their investigation of alleged renegade activities by a regimental comrade. The welcoming committee from the MoD had asked her what she was doing on British soil, and her future husband had told him that she wanted to see if England was 'really full of pricks like you'.

Davies smiled inwardly at the memory as he asked to speak to Razor.

'He's in Birmingham,' Hajrija told him. 'Seeing his mother and his football team. The two great loves of his life,' she added with a laugh.

Razor had always been close to his mother, Davies remembered. 'Can you give me her number?' he asked.

'Yes, but he won't be there. He's meeting friends before the match.'

Hajrija's English was almost as good as Razor's, Davies thought. Maybe even better. 'I'll call his mother and leave a message,' he said.

She gave him the number. 'What's it about?' she asked with her usual directness.

'Sorry, I can't tell you,' Davies said.

'That doesn't sound good.'

Davies didn't deny it. 'When is he due back?'

'He's driving back in the morning. I think he has a class at twelve.'

'Thanks.' He hung up, feeling worse for hearing the

anxiety in Hajrija's voice. He took a sip of malt, and punched out the Birmingham number she had given him.

The drive from Villa Park to the house his mother and stepfather had recently bought in Edgbaston took Razor Wilkinson about forty-five minutes. It was the first time he had seen Tottenham since November, and the first game they had lost since . . . November. Someone up there had obviously decided he was too damn happy these days. Bastard.

Razor pulled the car in behind his mum's Escort and noticed with pleasure that the downstairs lights were still on. He let himself in, and found her watching the opening credits of *Newsnight*.

'Jack's gone to bed,' she said. 'He's got an early start tomorrow.'

And he's probably also being tactful, Razor thought. One of the things he liked most about his new stepfather was that the man understood how close the bond was between mother and son. Since Razor's babyhood it had just been the two of them – the classic one-parent family of Tory demonology. And Razor had known a lot of kids with two parents who would have happily swapped them for the relationship he had with one.

He sat down and grinned at her.

'They lost,' she said.

'Yeah, but they looked good.'

She smiled at him. 'I remember you sulking for days when they lost.'

'I was only about six.'

'Twenty-six, more like. Hajrija phoned,' she added. 'Your boss wants to talk to you. Urgently.'

'The CO?'

'Lieutenant-Colonel Davies. He wanted you to call him as soon as you got in. The number's by the phone in the hall.'

Razor left her with Peter Snow and walked out into the hall, wondering what could be so urgent that it couldn't wait until the morning. If Hajrija had passed on the message, then she had to be all right.

He keyed the number, listened to eight rings, and was about to give up when a somewhat breathless Davies answered.

'Wilkinson, boss,' Razor replied. He could hear a woman's voice in the background, which both surprised and vaguely pleased him. He had always felt an instinctive liking for Barney Davies, and it was fairly common knowledge around the Regimental mess that the man's marriage break-up had turned him into a social recluse. Maybe he was coming out of his shell at last.

Or, then again, it might be a hooker. Or his mother.

'Something's come up,' the CO was saying. 'Remember the week you and Docherty spent in Guatemala in 1980?'

'Christ, not very well. I'd only been badged a few months. Why, what's happened?'

Davies told Razor exactly what Clarke had told him, and did his best to keep his doubts to himself. Before airing them, he wanted Razor's reaction. 'Would you be able to recognize this man?' he asked, hoping the answer would be no.

'Yeah, I don't see why not. We spent quite a lot of time with him. Even taught him how to play Cheat.'

'Did you like him?'

'I wouldn't say that. He was holding English hostages, and threatening to kill them.' He paused. 'Docherty sort of liked him, though,' he said.

Davies grunted. 'Somehow that doesn't surprise me.'

'What about Chris Martinson?' Razor asked.

'What about him?' Davies asked, surprised.

'He's in Guatemala.'

'He is? I had no idea. What the hell's he doing there?'

'There's a town there where you can do Spanish courses and live with a family while you're doing them. He's hoping for a field job with one of the charities when his term ends, and he wanted to bring his Spanish up to scratch.' Razor grunted. 'And no doubt he's doing some bird-watching while he's there.'

'How long has he been gone?'

'Two weeks, two and a half . . . I'm not sure. I think he's due back at the end of next week. He had a lot of leave piled up.'

'Ah,' Davies said, wondering how he could make use of the coincidence. 'Look,' he said, 'sleep on this, and I'll see you in my office when you get here in the morning.'

'OK, boss,' Razor said, wondering why the CO sounded so anxious. Maybe he'd forgotten to drop in at Boots on the way home to pick up some condoms. Or maybe he knew more about the situation in Guatemala than Razor did. Which wouldn't be difficult. He couldn't remember reading or seeing a single news item about the place in the past fifteen years.

He did remember the ruins where the negotiations had taken place. The two of them had driven there by jeep along the jungle road from Belize, stayed in a one-room inn which deserved a minus-five-star rating, and met with the terrorist leader on a square of grass surrounded by soaring stone temples. Tikal had been the name of the place. There had been monkeys in the trees, and huge red parrots zooming round in formation like dive-bombers, and those birds with the huge multicoloured beaks whose name he couldn't remember. Around dawn the mist had lingered in the trees, and one morning he and Docherty had climbed to the top of one of the temples and seen the tops of the others sticking out through the roof of mist like strange islands in a strange ocean.

He was only twenty-one then, not much more than a kid, and he supposed he hadn't really appreciated it.

'You OK?' his mother asked from the living-room doorway.

'Yeah, fine. It's just one more job that no one else can do.'

The moon had been gone for several minutes, and the luminous haze above the distant ridge-top was visibly fading. Tomás Xicay could almost feel the sighs of relief as true darkness enveloped the clearing where the *compas* were taking a ten-minute rest-stop. There was nothing but shadows around him, and the rustle of movement, and the whisper of conversation.

A hand came down on his shoulder. 'Is everything OK, Tomás?'

'*Sí, Commandante*,' he told the Old Man. He was tireder than tired, but then which of them wasn't? Except maybe the Old Man himself, who always seemed utterly indefatigable.

'Only a few weeks,' the Old Man said wryly, and moved on to encourage someone else.

Tomás smiled to himself in the dark. When, two months earlier, their current strategy had been agreed, that had been the crucial phrase. 'We must get them on the run, if only for a few weeks,' the Old Man had told the group leaders gathered that night on the hill outside Chichicastenango. 'Show the Army and the Americans that we are still alive, and that they are not immune to retribution.'

What would happen after those 'few weeks' no one knew for certain, but there was no doubt that the sort of aggressive tactics they had decided on would have a limited lifespan, because surprise always carried a diminishing return, and without it they would always be outgunned. And they knew that the longer they pursued these tactics the more certain it was that most of them would be killed.

As the column got back underway Tomás found himself wondering whether the Old Man ever had any doubts, and if so who it was he shared them with. Tomás at least had his sister, though being the man of the family he naturally tried to shield her from his more negative feelings. On his return from the city she had been quick to notice that something had upset him, and he had told her it was just seeing their relations, and the family memories they brought back. That had been true, but it was not the whole truth. During his days in the city he had seen their struggle in a different light, and it had disturbed him.

This column of *compas*, striding through the night forest, seemed so full of strength and rightness, so powerful . . . but there were only forty-four of them, and only the trees and the darkness shielded them, and not 150 kilometres away two million people were getting on with their daily lives oblivious to the guerrillas' very existence. In the city it was hard to believe that the Government could ever be toppled, that anything could shift the dead-weight of all that had gone before. It all seemed so permanent, so solid. Five hundred years' worth. And when Tomás thought about how much his people had suffered to keep their world alive, he found it hard to imagine the world of the Ladinos and the Yankees proving any less stubborn.

Still, no matter how much he might doubt their eventual triumph, he never doubted the need to continue with their struggle. What, after all, was the alternative? To accept the way things were? The poem in Tomás's pocket had the words for that: '. . . *it seems to me that it cannot be, that in this way, we are going nowhere. To survive so has no glory.*'

It had been the Old Man who had introduced him to the poetry of Pablo Neruda, a few months after their first meeting in the Mexican refugee camp. By then they had become firm friends – or perhaps more like father and son – but at the beginning Tomás had found it hard to take the older man seriously. His stories had seemed so outlandish, so much like comic-book adventures, that Tomás had taken him for the camp storyteller, more of an entertainer than a fighter.

In one story the Old Man had been taking some explosives to the guerrillas in the mountains, when he was stopped at an army roadblock. The soldiers were in a good mood that day, and only gave him a few bruises and burns before telling him he could continue on his way for no more than the price of his sack of beans. Unfortunately this was where he had hidden the explosives, so for an hour or more the Old Man pleaded and whined for the sack's return. Eventually the lieutenant in charge of the roadblock grew so sick of this incessant lament that he hurled the bag at the Old Man and told him to get lost. His one great achievement in life, the storyteller told his listeners, was not to recoil at the prospect of an explosion as the sack landed at his feet.

And then there was his favourite escape story. He had

been staying with comrades in Guatemala City, and alone in the house when the sound of vehicles approaching at high speed had alerted him. He had walked out into the front yard, picked up a broom and started sweeping, just as the lorries came hurtling down the street. They had screeched to a halt and disgorged running soldiers, all of whom raced straight past the Old Man into the house and started breaking furniture. The lieutenant in charge, who had been sent to arrest a notorious guerrilla leader, told him: 'Get the fuck out of here, old man!' He had accordingly shuffled off down the street.

Both these stories, Tomás had later found out, were true in every detail. The man he had taken for the camp story-teller was probably the most successful guerrilla leader in the history of Guatemala's forty-year civil war. And if anyone could 'get them on the run for a few weeks', then it was him.

3

Barney Davies dropped Jean off at the hospital where she worked, and reached his office before eight, feeling torn between post-coital bliss and pre-mission anxiety. The smile which bubbled up from the one kept fading into the frown caused by the other.

The briefings on the current situation in Guatemala, which had already been faxed from Whitehall, didn't do much for the smile. There was a lot of talk about that country's return to civilian democracy, a few pious generalities about increased respect for human rights, and a lot of waffle about the importance of maintaining stability throughout Central America. According to the Foreign Office mandarins, the existence of a Mayan Indian rebellion in the Mexican state of Chiapas made it all the more imperative that the alleged progress towards an acceptable peace in Guatemala be sustained.

Reading between the lines, Davies was not convinced. After finishing the report he stared morosely out of the window for several minutes, and then ordered a second cup of tea and his first rock cake of the day.

One way of reducing the risks involved in sending Razor into the lion's den, he had decided, was to send him in with company. The two men had got to know each other during the Bosnian business, and the mere fact that Razor had known that Chris Martinson was in Guatemala suggested at least a minimal level of continuing contact.

What the Guatemalans would think of it, Davies had no idea. Nor did he much care.

The tea arrived, together with a surprisingly friable rock cake.

The seventy-mile drive from Birmingham, most of it on motorways, took Razor about as many minutes. Driving was something he had always done well, and usually faster than this. But as Hajrija had tactfully pointed out, if all the other drivers had his judgement and reflexes then he could get away with driving like a lunatic. Until then . . .

He was getting older in more ways than one, Razor thought. Ten, fifteen years earlier, and the prospect of a mission like this would have had his body churning out adrenalin by the pint. His heart would have been leaping at the thought of getting away from Hereford and into action, away from routine and into the unknown. One voice in his brain was still singing this song, but only one, and it sounded more like an echo of his youth than a part of the man he now was. Other voices were dolefully reminding him that these overseas outings only ever looked good in prospect and retrospect, and were rarely anything other than terrifying at the time. This particular mission, so far as he could tell, looked about as inviting as a fortnight in Mogadishu. And on top of everything else he would be away from Hajrija for longer than he cared to think about.

By the time he reached Stirling Lines Razor was having trouble keeping in contact with the adventurer within.

Barney Davies greeted him with a wide smile and ordered

cups of tea on the intercom. Razor glanced at the photograph frame on the CO's desk, half expecting to find a new face inside it, but it still contained the familiar picture of his children. In the dim distant past another photograph had featured a wife.

'What exactly do they want me to do?' Razor asked, once the tea's arrival had signalled the start of business.

'As far as I know, simply identify the man who calls himself "El Espíritu", or "The Ghost".' Presumably he'll be in custody by then, though how they intend to catch him without knowing what he looks like seems a moot point.'

'And then?' Razor asked.

'You come home.'

Razor grunted. 'So we have no guarantee that . . .' He paused. 'Well, that they don't just take him out and have him shot on my say-so.'

'I wouldn't have thought they'd want that sort of publicity,' Davies said carefully.

Razor looked up, feeling the weight of doubt suddenly bearing down on him. 'Which might just mean that they'll wait until I'm on the plane home.'

Davies shrugged. 'Maybe. The US State Department told the Foreign Office that if the Guatemalan Army had a hundred suspects they would probably shoot the lot, just to make sure of getting the right man.'

'Bastards,' Razor murmured, leaving Davies unsure whether he meant the State Department, Foreign Office or Guatemalan Army. Probably all three, he decided.

'Look,' the CO said, deciding to lay some cards on the table. 'I don't like this any more than you do. The Guatemalans are leaning on the Yanks, and they're leaning on us, and it's you who'll pick up the tab . . .'

'Come back, Docherty, all is forgiven,' Razor muttered.

Davies uttered a silent prayer of thanks that Jamie Docherty was now living in Chile, and far removed from this mess. 'It seems to me,' he said, 'that there's two ways we can go with this. Either you can refuse outright to go . . .' He looked Razor straight in the eye. 'And if you do I'll back you all the way.'

'Thanks, boss, but . . .'

'Or you can go out there and play it by ear. When it comes to the crunch you'll have to decide for yourself whether you want to identify this man or not. By then you should have a much better idea of who and what you're dealing with. On both sides of the fence.'

'You mean, when the moment comes I just look through the guy with an innocent expression on my face,' Razor said, amused. 'I like it.'

'Not necessarily. We know the man kidnapped a whole tour party, and God knows what else he's got up to in the last fifteen years. He's no innocent, whatever else he is.'

'He must be pretty old by now,' Razor said. 'He looked like a pensioner in 1980.'

'Anyway,' Davies went on, 'I'm not sending you out there alone.'

'I was going . . .'

'Chris Martinson can keep you company.'

'Oh, great. But I was thinking about someone else. The wife has always wanted to see Guatemala for some reason, and . . .'

'I don't think . . .'

'Only as a tourist, of course. She can do her own thing while I bond with the Guatemalan Army. She could maybe open the odd fête, if the Guatemalans ask her.'

Davies grinned in spite of himself. 'I don't know . . .'

'Maybe it's only an old Yugoslav custom, but she thinks men on diplomatic missions often take their wives along, with all expenses paid by the grateful hosts.'

The CO laughed. 'I can't wait to hear what the Foreign Office will say,' he said, reaching for the phone.

It took five minutes for the secretary to locate Martin Clarke, but far less time for Davies to lose his temper. 'If you are not prepared to ask the Guatemalans to accept a two-man team then you can go and look for help somewhere else,' he told Clarke. 'I am not prepared to send a single soldier, no matter how experienced, into a potential combat situation without any reliable backup.'

'I am not interested in debating the issue,' Clarke said.

'Then just get on with arranging what I asked for,' Davies said, and slammed down the phone.

Razor raised his eyebrows.

'He'll call back in a few minutes,' Davies said, with a confidence which he only half felt. It was kind of exhilarating, though, telling one of Her Majesty's Ministers where to get off.

And it worked. Clarke was back on the line in less than five minutes, sounding chagrined but humble. The Guatemalans didn't quite understand the necessity, he said, but they were happy to provide hospitality for as many Britons as came.

'Good,' Davies said. 'Please inform them that Sergeant Wilkinson will also be bringing his wife, who is eager to visit their beautiful country. They will need accommodation, and so will Sergeant Martinson. He is already in Guatemala, in Antigua.' He read out the address. 'If the relevant authorities can liaise with Martinson, he can meet the Wilkinsons at the airport on Sunday. Oh, and we'll need a ticket for Mrs Wilkinson on the same flight as her husband.'

'Anything else?' Clarke asked coldly.

'No, I don't think so,' Davies said, and put the phone down. He looked across at Razor, who was grinning at him, and looking not much more than half his thirty-six years. Davies smiled back, determined not to offer any outward display of the sudden sense of foreboding in his heart.

The news that the British had agreed to send their soldier reached Guatemala City soon after dawn, and an eager Alvaro was waiting to inform Serrano of the good tidings when the latter arrived at the G-2 offices in the Palacio Nacional.

'Good,' Serrano said, stirring sugar into the coffee which had just been brought to his desk.

'He will join up with the man in Antigua, the one we knew about,' Alvaro added. 'And he is bringing his wife.'

Serrano was pleased. 'Excellent,' he said. 'That must mean that no pressure has been put on him. If he is bringing his wife he must be happy to come. He will be a good witness.'

'I thought of putting them in the Pan-American Hotel,' Alvaro said. 'Tourists seem to like it.'

'They like it because it is comfortable, but not so luxurious that the streets outside make them feel guilty,' Serrano said. 'A good choice,' he added.

'Thank you, sir.'

Serrano sipped appreciatively at the dark coffee. 'Has there been any progress in the business of finding El Espíritu?' he asked, knowing full well that if there had been he would have been the first to know.

'Nothing definite yet, but the net is being drawn in.'

Serrano allowed himself a thin smile. 'Let's hope the little shit is in it.'

The sun was sinking behind the twin peaks of Fuego and Acatenango as Chris approached his lodgings. Like most of the houses in Antigua, the Martínez family residence wasn't much to look at from the outside, offering just a bare wall painted pastel yellow, with two small windows protected by wrought-iron grilles. But once through the gate the visitor found himself in an exquisite courtyard, decorated with palms and flowering pink bougainvillaea, and surrounded by cool, shuttered rooms.

From one of these rooms Chris could hear two voices which had become increasingly familiar over the past two and a half weeks; they belonged to Clara and Romero, the leading characters in the family's favourite soap opera. *Costa del Oro* was supposedly made in Colombia, though Chris had never noticed anything which reminded him of his own trip to that country. The programme was basically an Hispanic *Baywatch*, with even flimsier swimsuits, acting and story-lines. The Martínez family adored it.

He was waved into the only empty seat, next to sixteen-year-old Maria, whose life seemed to revolve around flirting with whoever was at hand, and whom Chris found worryingly attractive. This evening, though, she was too engrossed in the TV show to nestle up to him.

Chris watched it too, feeling pleased that he understood more or less everything that was being said, right down to the occasional – and probably unintentional – ironic nuances. His time in Antigua had certainly delivered the goods as far as his Spanish was concerned, and he had even grown rather fond of his hosts. In many ways they reminded him of an English family – only the names of the soap operas had been changed.

The day's episode ended with a cliff-hanger which made Chris nostalgic for the subtlety of *Neighbours*, and left the Martínezes in temporary shock. Señora Martínez recovered first, and headed for the kitchen, announcing over her shoulder that dinner would be in half an hour.

'There has been a call for you,' Maria told Chris, fixing her deep-black eyes on him.

'From who?' Chris asked.

'Your embassy in Guatemala City,' Señor Martínez told him. 'They want you to call them back. Please, use our telephone.'

Chris did so, and was put through to the Military Attaché, Ben Manley, with whom he had once served in the Green Howards. Manley relayed the new orders from Hereford, half sarcastically adding that it sounded 'like fun'.

'Doesn't it just,' Chris agreed wryly.

For the next couple of hours he put the whole business to the back of his mind, and concentrated on enjoying his dinner. After he had helped with the dishes – something which still astonished the whole family – he announced he was going for a walk, and then dealt Maria a crushing blow by refusing to ask for her company. He needed to do some thinking, he told her. She gave him a persecuted look.

Once outside, Chris began wandering aimlessly through Antigua's network of streets, feeling dismayed by the news. He told himself it would be good to see Razor and Hajrija, and that there seemed every likelihood he would now get to see parts of the country which were well off the tourist track. Who knew? – he might even find the twitcher's holy grail, a quetzal in the wild.

It wasn't enough. He felt almost cheated, and realized that although he still had two months of his final term to serve, he had begun to think and feel as if the SAS was already behind him.

He had been a good soldier – he was certain of that – but being a soldier, and an SAS soldier at that, had always been a means to an end for him, not an end in itself. It had given him the scope to stretch himself, and to see the wild parts of the world in a way which the tourist or even the seasoned traveller never could. There was no adventure-holiday company yet which offered a week-long hike out of Colombia, across mountains and through jungle, with the forces of a drug cartel and the national army on your tail.

But after Bosnia things hadn't been the same. Maybe it had been the mission itself, or maybe he had just outgrown one way of looking at himself and the world. Damien Robson had died there, making Joss Wynwood and himself the only remaining survivors of the Colombian mission. That was chilling enough, but not the main reason for his change of heart. In Bosnia he and Razor – both of whom had chosen medicine as their first SAS specialization – had spent as much time looking after people as they had fighting. There had been the women from the Serb brothel, the children injured in the shelling of Zavik. He and Docherty had been round Sarajevo's City Hospital, and witnessed the incredible dedication of people working in near-impossible conditions.

Back in England he had decided that there were other ways to travel and to serve than with the SAS. He had been quite happy to serve out the remainder of his three-year term. The work was rarely boring and there were always new opportunities to learn. Some of these – like the helicopter pilot's course he had recently begun – would provide him with skills that were bound to be useful in the sort of Third World situations where he expected to find his civilian future.

What he had not anticipated was that anyone would ask him to take up arms again, much less send him out on loan to an army notorious for its murderous cruelty.

The MI5 report was waiting on Martin Clarke's desk when he arrived back that evening from a day-trip to Brussels. Placing the miniature hamper of Belgian chocolates to one side – he had forgotten Valentine's Day the previous year, and decided to shop in advance this time – he took the file across to the armchair by the window and started to read.

Darren James Wilkinson was born on 6 February 1958, which made him almost thirty-seven. And, as Clarke's wife Sarah would have told him, an Aquarius. He had been raised in Islington and Walthamstow by his hospital nurse mother, and attended the local comprehensives. The name Highbury Grove rang a bell. Wasn't that the school Rhodes Boyson had been headmaster of? God help the pupils, Clarke thought.

Wilkinson had clearly shown no aptitude for study. He had left school in the summer of 1974, and spent the next eighteen months moving from job to job. He had been out of the country several times during that period, mostly as a travelling football supporter, but there had also been two three-month stints as a barman in Marbella. He had joined the Army soon after his eighteenth birthday. After four years' service with the Welsh Guards he had applied to join the SAS, and satisfied all the entrance requirements with flying colours.

No doubt his experiences as a football hooligan had come in handy, Clarke thought sourly.

But he had to admit that the man had an excellent service record. His first important job had been the one in Guatemala, and though he had obviously played a subordinate role, he had been commended for his performance. Two years later there had been the business in Argentina, which Clarke already knew about. The only new information in this regard concerned Wilkinson's subsequent arrest, along with fellow-trooper Stewart Nevis, on a charge of being drunk and disorderly in the Chilean town of Puerto Natales. The two men had apparently defaced a local statue and given the locals an impromptu concert at two in the morning.

'Once a football hooligan, always a football hooligan,' Clarke murmured to himself.

Still, Wilkinson had been promoted to corporal almost immediately, and raised to the rank of sergeant five years later, when he joined the staff of the Regiment's Training Wing. From then until the Bosnia mission early in 1993 he had hardly been out of the UK.

Clarke had never been privy to the details of the affair in Bosnia, and after reading the report's account he could see why his superiors had not been eager to publicize the matter. The SAS team had been sent in to investigate rumours that one of their own colleagues was running a private war in the Bosnian mountains, and if necessary to extract him by force. Instead of doing so, they had rescued about fifty women from a Serb prison, done everything but assist their renegade colleague in his private war, and then ignored direct orders to bring the man out, escorting a truckload of wounded children to safety instead.

The report attributed this wilful insubordination to the team commander, the now-retired Sergeant James Docherty, but as far as Clarke could see no action had been taken against either him or any of the others. The SAS had simply closed ranks around the matter, as if the Regiment was a law unto itself. Which it probably was, Clarke thought. He was still smarting from the way its Commanding Officer had addressed him a few days earlier.

What had Wilkinson's contribution to the affair been? Clarke wondered. Had he argued with Docherty, simply followed orders, or even encouraged him? There was no way of knowing. But it was Wilkinson who had married the Bosnian woman that the SAS team brought out with them; Wilkinson who had called the MoD official at RAF Brize Norton 'a prick'.

Clarke sighed and stared out at the London night. There didn't seem much doubt that the man was prone to insubordination. But at least he hadn't been in any trouble since the Bosnian business. According to the report he had suffered from persistent nightmares for a while, but a few visits to the Regiment's 'psychiatric counsellor' had apparently put him back together again. Anyway, he was the one the Guatemalans wanted. They could damn well keep him in order.

Ten minutes later Clarke began telling his contact in the US State Department that there were few finer examples of British soldiering at its brilliant best than Sergeant Darren Wilkinson of 22 SAS.

* * *

A solitary bird suddenly began to sing, and after what seemed only a momentary pause, another thousand joined in. Emelia Xicay lay flat on her stomach in the tall grass above the road and listened. For a few minutes the nerves which always preceded an action were banished, and she smiled with unalloyed pleasure. At times like this she always felt truly blessed – this, just as much as the horrors and the sadnesses, was her birthright as a Mayan Indian. Here in the mist she felt herself enveloped by the damp richness of the earth and trees, carried along by the song of the birds. She belonged in the natural world, the way so few foreigners seemed to do.

At such times she felt almost sorry for the Ladinos, who seemed to have no such sense. But not all of them, she reminded herself sternly. Tomás said some understood life and the earth the same way their own people did. He had Ladino friends, and she would too, once she could speak to them fluently in their own language.

She thought about the city, and wondered if she would ever see it. Tomás had told her about it, of course, and so had Francisco, but she suspected that both brother and lover had censored their accounts, as if they was trying to protect her from all the many evils which befell their people there.

She hadn't thought about Francisco for several days, she realized. It was almost a year now since his death in the army ambush.

She turned her mind back to the city. She didn't want to live there, just to see it. The biggest towns she had ever visited were Santa Cruz del Quiche in Guatemala and San Cristobal de las Casas in Mexico. They had lived just outside the latter for a while, and Emelia had sold woven bracelets to the tourists in the town's main square with several other refugee children. She could remember lifting up her wares to the smoked-glass windows of the big buses, the pale white hands reaching down with money.

The men on the road below were speaking to each other in low voices, and Emelia thought she caught Tomás's Tzutujil accent among them. The first hint of light was showing in the mist away to her left, above the deep and hidden valley which carried the road up from Cunen.

He should be leaving about now, if he was leaving at all. According to the reports of the *compas* assigned to the task of watching over him, Morales was a creature of rigid habits, and so far there had been no sign that the fate of Major Muñoz had persuaded him to deviate from any of his normal routines. Each Friday morning he left the command HQ in Cunen and drove across these mountains to the subordinate outpost at El Desengaño, where he gathered intelligence of the previous week's operations and planned those for the following week. There seemed no practical reason for this journey by road – radio communication would have served just as well, or a helicopter could have covered the same distance in a tenth of the time – but Morales liked to impose himself in person, and from all accounts he loved to drive, and to be seen driving, his new Cherokee Chief station wagon.

And in any case, the Old Man had said, what did Morales have to worry about? His friends in the neighbouring command would have told him the guerrillas were cowering in the forest, somewhere inside the closing ring of troops thirty kilometres to the west. True, they hadn't actually been seen for several days, but there was no way they could have broken out.

Emelia hoped the Old Man was right. He usually was.

It was getting steadily lighter now, and holes were beginning to appear in the mist, drifting holes, like floating windows. On the road below she could now see the seven *compañeros* in their costumes, and the glass cabinet lying on its side. At the foot of the grassy bank Jorge was setting light to the second of two censers packed with incense. Smoke from the first was already wafting up to reinforce the mist, and carrying the sweet, acrid smell to Emelia's nostrils.

With both censers burning, the group below settled into stillness, like a film frozen on a single frame, waiting to be restarted. Emelia lay there with the rifle, watching the mist slowly clear, hearing the chorus of birdsong gradually abate, feeling the cold edge drawn from the air by the rising sun. Ten minutes went by, and twenty, and thirty, and then she could hear the sound of vehicles. As it grew steadily louder the tableau on the road below sprang back into life. She swallowed nervously, and tried not to grip the rifle too tightly.

As he guided the Cherokee Chief up the steep incline, Captain Juan García Morales was thinking about what to do with his new-found wealth. He had just inherited around 200,000 quetzals from a great-uncle, and those closest to him could not agree as to how he should invest it. His wife wanted him to buy property in Florida, but his father was advising Lake Atitlán. Morales instinctively preferred the Florida option, but he had to admit that his father was rarely wrong when it came to such matters. 'You get yourself a shoreline on the most beautiful lake in the world,' he had told his son, 'and in five years the value will multiply tenfold or more. Once we have the Indian business finally settled you won't be able to see that lake for investors.'

He was probably right. After all, Lake Atitlán had continued to draw tourists no matter how bad things got. And if they could move the Indians back from the shoreline, and simply bus them in to work in the hotels and sell the stuff the tourists loved so much, then the sky was probably the limit. The place could become another Acapulco.

Morales steered the car round a bend in the slope, and drove through a small but stubborn patch of mist, emerging just above a sheer drop of several hundred metres. He could feel the nervousness of the soldiers beside and behind him, and rather enjoyed the sensation. In the rear-view mirror he was watching for the following jeep to materialize out of the mist when figures loomed out of another patch almost directly in front of him.

As he applied the brakes Morales instinctively reached for his holstered automatic, and then brought his hand away empty. It was only a bunch of Indian holy men – *cofradías*, they were called; he was always running into them on the roads, carrying their holy dummies to one of their countless festivals. And this bunch of idiots had managed to drop their dummy – he could see it, a child's version of the Virgin Mary, lying face down on the road, next to the overturned cabinet in which they had been carrying it.

One of the old men was walking towards the Cherokee, probably to apologize for getting in the Army's way. Morales took note of the ridiculous costume – the knee-length shorts and the rag wound round the man's head – and wondered why the tourists found this anything other than pathetic.

The weather-beaten face of the old man was smiling apologetically at him as he approached the car window. And then, as if by magic, a revolver was boring into Morales's ear.

'If you want to live another second,' the old man said in perfect Spanish, 'tell your men to leave the jeep without their weapons.'

Razor closed the guidebook and tried stuffing it into the pocket on the back of the seat in front of him. This was not easy, as the slim pocket already contained his Walkman, two airline magazines, instructions on how to behave if the airliner suddenly plummeted 30,000 feet into the Atlantic, a Ruth Rendell mystery and a half-empty quarter-bottle of Sauvignon Blanc.

He had learnt one thing from Hajrija's guidebook – the rest of Guatemala had little in common with the bit he had visited in 1980. The ruins of Tikal were situated in the thinly populated northern half of the country, a mostly flat area of jungles and swamps, but most of the country's people lived either on the Pacific coastal plain or in the vast swath of mountains, plateaux and valleys which formed the country's backbone. It sounded like Chris Martinson's descriptions of Colombia, and like nothing Razor had ever seen.

In the window seat next to him Hajrija was happily giggling at *Blackadder*, which was showing on the tiny screen. Razor reckoned he'd already seen the episode about half a dozen times, and watching the final scenes without the benefit of headphones, he found he could lip-read the dialogue.

He sneaked a glance at Hajrija's happy face, and wondered yet again at his luck in not only finding but also holding on to her. Her lustrous black hair was pulled loosely back in a ponytail, making her look younger than usual, and her high cheekbones were faintly glistening in the sunlight. The first time he had seen her, standing in the corridor of the Sarajevo Holiday Inn, those cheekbones had jutted from a face made gaunt by stress and an inadequate diet.

The credits started to roll, and she took off the headphones. 'The English are completely crazy,' she said, readjusting her hair.

'It's all we have left,' Razor said. He retrieved the guidebook from the crowded pocket. 'What first made you want to go to Guatemala?' he asked.

She lifted both shoulders in the familiar shrug. 'I don't remember,' she said. 'You know how it is – some countries just seem appealing. Some don't. Maybe I saw some pictures when I was a child, or a programme on TV. I can't remember. But I always wanted to see Lake Atitlán. I mean, how many big lakes are there with volcanoes all around them? And I grew up in mountains. The air is so clear in places like that, and the colours. I love it. I want to see Peru as well, and Kashmir.'

She was switching channels as she spoke, in search of further entertainment. 'Are you going to watch a movie?' she asked.

'Don't think so.'

'Are you OK?' she asked, turning towards him, feeling slightly worried. He didn't seem his usual ebullient self.

'Fine. I just don't like watching things on a screen the size of a postage stamp.'

'You should have your eyes tested,' she said.

He nodded and grinned.

Satisfied, she put the headphones back on and left him

to the guidebook. Razor squeezed it back into the pocket and sat back with his eyes closed, thinking how strange it was to be heading out on a job like this with her beside him. Still, this whole trip had a strange feeling to it. For one thing the CO had driven them to Gatwick in person, which had to be a first. And for most of the journey Razor had had the feeling Davies was biting his tongue rather than saying what was on his mind. His last words had been: 'Remember, if you feel the need to press the ejector button, just do it. And we'll just have to deal with the political fall-out.'

That was all very well, Razor thought, but he preferred Jamie Docherty's epigram: 'When the shit hits the fan, it's too late to turn the fan off.'

What the hell. He looked at his watch, and saw that the Tottenham versus Blackburn game was an hour away from kick-off. Just his luck, he thought – the day they played the League leaders and he had to miss it. If there was ever a nuclear war, Razor was convinced it would come with Tottenham one point short of their first League title since the Middle Ages.

He closed his eyes again, and let the hum of the jet engines lull him into sleep.

Chris Martinson and Ben Manley sat in the coffee bar which overlooked the arrival hall at Guatemala City's Aurora International Airport, and watched a plane-load of American tourists and returning Ladino families pluck their luggage from the carousel.

'Is this guy a friend or just a brother-in-arms?' Manley asked.

'A friend, I suppose,' Chris said. He had always been something of a loner, and since Eddie Wilshaw's death in

Colombia he had got used to the idea of not having friends, but over the past couple of years he had felt closer to Razor than anyone else, male or female.

'Well, that should help,' Manley said. 'But these Guatemalan Army guys, they're not half as bad as the press they get. Most of the officers come from good families, and most of them have been trained in the States. There are a few psychos, like there are in any army, ours included.'

'What about G-2?' Chris asked.

'They had a bad reputation in the eighties, and I suppose it's still not good. But you won't have to deal with them. We've been promised this is a strictly army affair.'

Chris sipped at his coffee, wondering who Manley was trying to kid. There didn't seem much left of the wide-eyed innocent Chris had first known in the Green Howards. Manley was a fellow East Anglian and another bird-watcher, and they had spent a lot of time together in those days, both in England and Germany. But their career paths had diverged, and Manley seemed to have acquired the blinkers necessary for following his. He hadn't changed, simply narrowed his focus.

Maybe he had himself, Chris thought, but he didn't think so. 'What's the social life like around here?' he asked.

'Restricted. Just the other embassies, really. Most of the locals you meet are too rich to notice you. There's only the junior officers, really, and some of them are OK. They know where the action is, anyway.'

'And the women?' Chris asked.

'Difficult. This is a Catholic country, so any female over fourteen is either a wife, a Virgin Mary or a tart. The only real exceptions are students, and you have to be pretty careful what you're getting into with them as well.'

'What about the Indians?'

Manley snorted. 'Another world altogether. It's like apartheid,' he added, without any apparent moral judgement. 'The two worlds just don't mix.'

Except when it comes to hiring servants, Chris thought to himself, just as a growing roar outside announced the arrival of another flight.

'That'll be the Miami flight,' Manley said, getting to his feet. 'We'd better get down there.'

Razor and Hajrija were still on the plane when a smiling young man in a uniform arrived to escort them through the entry formalities. These consisted of a single brief conversation between their young man and another uniform in a booth, who thereupon attacked both their passports with a fiercesome-looking stamp. Their bags, which included two SAS uniforms and two Browning High Power 9mm semi-automatics with extra magazines, had already reached the arrival hall, where Chris Martinson and another man were standing guard over it.

'Look what the wind blew in,' Chris said.

'It's good to see you too,' Razor said. 'I was wondering who was going to carry the luggage.'

Manley thanked the Guatemalan and led the other three across the cavernous hall and out through the exit. On the other side of the road Hertz and Budget car rental offices sat beneath a huge hoarding advertising Lucky Strike cigarettes. 'I love exotic countries,' Razor said, as Manley opened up the embassy limousine.

The Wilkinsons slumped into the back seat. 'The hotel's good,' Chris said from the front, just as a huge roar sounded to their left and two Chinook military helicopters loomed above the row of offices and lifted away out of sight. They reminded Razor of *Apocalypse Now*. Nice omen, he thought.

A few moments later they were passing under an old stone aqueduct and entering the city. At the first major intersection a large building announced itself as Chuck E Cheese's Centre Mall, and behind it were ranged several residential high-rises. It all looked like the Lea Bridge Road translated into Spanish, Razor decided.

Things improved as Manley turned the car down a broad, tree-lined boulevard. There were donkey rides for children in the wide central reservation, and one local entrepreneur was doing a roaring trade in Batman T-shirts. Most of the buildings lining the road seemed to be either hotels or offices, and all of them flew the sky-blue and white national flag.

'There's a logic to their flag,' Manley told them. 'The blue on either side symbolizes the Pacific and Atlantic, and the white in between is the peace the conquistadors brought to the land. Hence the quetzal holding the olive branch.'

Irony, blindness, or plain conceit? Chris wondered. Probably a combination of the last two.

'One of the more endearing things about this place,' Manley was saying, 'is the number of rich crazies it seems to produce. People with more money than sense. Look at this church on the left . . .'

They all stared out at the bizarre building, which seemed to have been constructed as a monument to several different architectural traditions. It looked like a cross between the Kremlin, Westminster Abbey and a Venetian palace.

'There's a copy of the Eiffel Tower a couple of streets over,' Manley went on, 'and in one of the parks there's a relief map of the country the size of a tennis court. This is a strange town.'

'I see what you mean,' Razor said, as they drove past a huge statue of two fighting bulls. 'What's that?' he asked, as they passed a large, castle-like building, complete with battlements and armed guards.

'Police headquarters.'

'Figures.'

They passed under a railway bridge and across a wide open space between parks before burrowing into a narrower street festooned with advertisements.

'This is the oldest part of the city,' Manley said.

It looked more interesting, but not a lot more welcoming. There didn't seem to be many people on the streets, and most of those seemed to be hurrying along, heads bowed down, as if keen to reach home before something bad happened. There was something distinctly shabby about the capital of Guatemala, Razor thought. And perhaps sinister as well.

'Most of the guidebooks tell tourists not to waste any time here,' Hajrija said, as if sharing his thoughts.

The hotel, though, was as good as Chris claimed. A small corridor led into a covered courtyard, whose walls were lined with samples of the woven designs of different Mayan tribes. Razor and Hajrija sat down at one of the tables and looked at them while Manley and Chris checked them in.

Having done his job, the embassy man left, and a hotel employee showed them to their rooms. The doors were numbered, and on the wall beside each one there was a small painting of a Mayan god. 'That's Ixchel, the Goddess of Medicine,' Hajrija said, looking at the one by their door.

Razor was impressed.

'Some people sleep on planes, some read,' she told him.

'I'm going to have a stroll around the main square,' Chris announced. 'You two probably want to get some rest.'

'Yeah . . .' Razor began.

'We'll come,' Hajrija said. 'I need to stretch my legs after all that sitting.'

'How far is it?' Razor asked hopefully.

'Just round the corner,' Chris said.

Five minutes later they were crossing the road which surrounded the square, and entering an expanse the size of two football pitches. At the end away to their right a large, twin-towered, cream-coloured church seemed to glow against the darkening sky, while directly ahead of them a much larger building of similar vintage was already brooding in the twilight shadows. More noteworthy than either, the square itself was packed with people, some selling a variety of wares but most simply taking the early-evening air. The majority were in Western dress, but there was also a significant number of people wearing traditional Indian costume. After the half-empty streets of their drive from the airport this much life seemed almost intoxicating.

The three of them wandered through the throng in the general direction of the church, past women cooking corn-cobs on small charcoal braziers, men hawking bursts of candyfloss that were displayed like trophies on large wooden crosses, and more women sitting with little piles of herbs arranged on cotton sheets. Children sucked lollipops, chewed on tortillas and drank from the elegant glass Coca-Cola bottles which Razor remembered from his childhood. A tide of noise, of conversation and laughter and children crying, rolled over them. A series of overlapping smells rose and faded in their nostrils.

A rapid-fire succession of deafening explosions almost

made them jump out of their skins, but there was only excitement on the faces all around, and the clouds of smoke billowing into the air above the western end of the square came from nothing more threatening than fireworks. The threesome grinned sheepishly at each other, and joined the crowd in its drift towards the scene of the action.

Another salvo of firecrackers rent the air, noisier than any of them had ever heard, and almost immediately two rockets screamed into the sky, exploding with equally deafening effect some fifty metres above the crowd. The sticks fell back to earth, causing those at risk below to scatter with screeches of mock alarm.

A procession was now emerging through the whirling smoke which covered the road. First came an altar boy, swinging a large tin brazier of smoking frankincense, and then twenty or so males, some looking no older than adolescents, carrying a huge, flower-decked bier on their shoulders. Above the flowers, swaying with the motion of the bier, loomed a half-size model of the crucified Christ. The cross was gold, the figure black.

Behind the bier came a band, all brass and drums.

'I wonder where they're going,' Razor wondered out loud.

'I'd guess the church,' Chris said. He had seen a similar, albeit smaller, procession in Antigua the previous weekend. 'They usually start and finish where the statues live.'

'It's wonderful,' Hajrija said, her eyes shining.

'Yeah,' Razor agreed. It was, although he was damned if he knew why. The music and the smoke and the costumes and the swaying Christ – a world unto itself, a foreign world.

Then his eyes caught the soldiers on the other side of

the road, standing in a group of four by the entrance to the large building. They were all wearing smartly pressed uniforms and polished leather boots. Each was cradling a dull black Uzi. None looked older than sixteen.

'What is that building?' he asked Hajrija.

'The National Palace,' she said. 'The guidebook says it was built in the 1930s as a gift to the people.'

Razor grunted. The expressions on the faces of the boy-soldiers seemed a potent mixture of envy, fear and contempt. And as if to emphasize the divide, at that moment the sounds of celebration were drowned out by the rising roar of a military transport plane, flying low across the square like a huge black bird.

'Someone's telling us all something,' Chris murmured.

The band played on, the black Christ continued its homeward journey, and the rockets reclaimed the sky from the enemy. The three of them walked back across the rapidly darkening square towards their hotel, saying little.

Once back in their room, Razor decided to take a shower, and a few moments later Hajrija joined him. There was a smile on her face, but something else in her eyes, and they clung to each other in the streaming hot water, both aroused and disturbed by what they had witnessed. And as the fierceness of this feeling slowly transmuted into the more familiar blend of love and lust, they joined together with a passionate urgency which recalled their first night together in Zavik, more than two years before.

Later, with Hajrija asleep in his arms, Razor found himself remembering the favourite book of his youth, Tolkien's *Lord of the Rings*, and wondering whether the two of them had fallen into a land of fantasy, where a sense of wonder and of evil had survived in undiluted form.

4

At ten o'clock the following morning the promised escort arrived at the Pan-American Hotel. The young officer, clean-shaven with deep-brown eyes and a friendly smile, introduced himself to the two SAS men as Lieutenant Ricardo Velázquez Gómez. 'But call me Ricky,' he added, taking each of their right hands between both of his own.

Razor wondered whether to insist on their speaking the local language, but decided that the lieutenant's English was probably better than his own Spanish. 'Where exactly are we going?' he asked as they left the hotel and walked across the road to where a black limousine with smoked-glass windows was gently purring. The driver, who was in plain clothes, eyed the SAS uniforms with interest.

'We are going to the home of Colonel Serrano in Zona 14,' Gómez said. 'He is in charge of this business and he thought it would be a more comfortable place for getting acquainted . . . more informal, yes?'

'Fine by us,' Razor said, and followed Chris into the back seat.

The limousine moved away smoothly, with both SAS men conscious of the stares pursuing them from the pavements. Gómez turned round in the front seat and gave them another friendly smile. 'I have worked with the American Special

Forces,' he said. 'Delta Force and the Rangers. I have good friends there, you know. But even some of my American friends tell me the SAS is the best. So I am pleased to be your liaison.'

Razor grinned. 'Pleasure's mutual,' he said.

'I have read about the Princes Gate. And Las Malvinas . . . the Falklands, I mean.' He grinned. 'And the operation in Gibraltar. I would like to hear your opinion of these things when we have some time. If it is allowed.'

'It's allowed,' Razor admitted.

'Are you stationed here in Guatemala City?' Chris asked.

'Yes. It is the best place to be. Not for this,' Gómez added, taking in the seedy-looking streets of the market district with a wave of his arm. 'You will see – where we are going it is a very nice place, very civilized.'

As the limousine droned down the wide avenue, past the castellated police headquarters and the statue of the fighting bulls, the smoked glass displayed the Guatemalan capital in a sinister twilight. If the authorities spent their lives looking through windows like this, Chris thought, then no wonder paranoia was rampant.

At the Chuck E Cheese intersection they turned left, away from the direction of the airport, and quickly found themselves slowing for a control booth.

'Is this a restricted area?' Razor asked Gómez, once the young officer had cleared them through.

'No, it is only a precaution against terrorism,' Gómez replied. 'There are many embassies in this area, and the terrorists like to make big news, get on CNN. And the BBC, of course.'

The SAS men were not convinced. It felt more like a

private estate than an ordinary district of the city. The streets were virtually empty of either pedestrians or traffic, and what could be seen of the houses behind the high, stucco walls and wrought-iron gates suggested money – lots of it. And the razor wire which adorned the tops of the walls made clear the intention to hang on to every last penny. Above the gleaming coils the heads of luxuriant palms basked in the morning sun, and large white satellite dishes reached up for their signals.

It was no wonder the bastards had built their little enclave so close to the airport, Razor thought. If the revolution came they wouldn't have so far to run.

'There is the Swiss Embassy,' Gómez said, pointing out a villa on their left. Through the tall gates they could see a swimming pool surrounded by flowering bougainvillaea, a gardener hard at work. 'It is nice, yes?' Gómez said. 'One day maybe I buy for my family,' he added with a boyish grin.

Another fifty metres, and the limousine turned in towards another pair of gates. Gómez left the car to use the intercom, and was no sooner back in his seat than the gates swung wide. They followed a curving drive through a stand of royal palms and came to a halt outside one of the most beautiful houses either SAS man had ever seen. Set on a slight slope, the one-storey, white-stucco villa seemed to exist on several levels, as if it were a series of rooms caught in the act of cascading downhill. Wrought-ironwork adorned the windows, and gorgeous flowering plants clung to the walls. In front of the house water rippled from an intricately carved stone fountain.

Two men were waiting on the front steps, both of them in army uniform. Gómez introduced the more thickset of the two as Colonel Cabrera. He was probably not much more than thirty-five, with neatly parted black hair and a short moustache. He was darker-skinned than either Gómez or Serrano, taller than the average Guatemalan, and looked as though he spent considerable time and energy keeping his body in trim. His welcome was jovial enough, but his eyes seemed uncertain, as if he needed a clearer statement of the visitors' status.

Behind Cabrera stood their host, the thinner Colonel Serrano. The two men might hold the same rank, but it didn't take the SAS men long to realize which of them was in charge. There was nothing overt – Cabrera didn't defer and Serrano didn't patronize – but there was still no room for doubt. Cabrera was just a soldier, which in this country might well mean no more than a well-connected bully in uniform. Serrano, his black eyes like burn-holes in a gaunt face, was obviously one of the men who took the real decisions. Intelligence most likely, despite the Guatemalan Government's promise that this would be a strictly military affair.

Lines like that were hard to draw any more, Razor thought. He and Chris had been shepherded into a spacious living room, where several comfortable sofas and armchairs were arranged around a woven rug.

'I took the liberty of ordering coffee,' Serrano said.

'Thank you,' Razor said, thinking about the football magazine which had been left lying, a little too artfully, on the coffee table. He had the strong sense that they were already being manipulated.

'My son loves football,' Serrano said in English. 'He still talks about your Gary Lineker in the World Cup.'

'Yeah, great player,' Razor agreed, manfully resisting the temptation to get drawn in.

A maid arrived with the coffee, but Serrano saw to the pouring and distribution himself, rather in the manner of someone orchestrating a children's tea party. The coffee was deliciously strong.

'How was your flight?' Serrano asked Razor.

'Fine. I slept most of the way.'

'And you have been enjoying your time in Antigua?' he asked Chris.

'Very much.'

'Well, if there is anything else we can arrange for you, any sights you would like to see, please inform Lieutenant Gómez. I'm sure he will be able to fit it into the schedule somehow.'

'Thank you.'

Serrano waved away the gratitude. 'We appreciate your help in this matter, believe me. It may not seem an important matter to people outside our country, but these are crucial times here, and any set-back to the peace negotiations could be serious, not only for us but for the whole region. You are aware of the current situation in Mexico?'

'We've got a rough idea,' Razor conceded.

Serrano leaned forward in his seat. 'The so-called Zapatistas are basically left-wing agitators from Mexico City who are using the Indians' grievances to further their own aims. And they have strong links with terrorists in this country who seek the same ends. At the moment their main anxiety is that my government will reach an accord with the Indian groups and, as you English say, pull the carpet out from under their feet.'

Razor took a sip of coffee. Gómez had listened to Serrano's pitch with dog-like devotion, but Cabrera seemed bored by the whole business. 'How does our man fit into all this?' Razor asked.

Serrano smiled ruefully. 'Until recently we thought this man was long since dead, but after he claimed responsibility for several recent outrages a full investigation was mounted, and it now seems that he has spent several years across the border in Chiapas, plotting with the Zapatistas. His group wants no accommodation with the Government, no peace, so he is an outlaw even among the other guerrilla factions, who do want peace.' Serrano looked sadly at the two Englishmen. 'This country has been at war for far too long,' he said. 'That is why we are a poor country, despite all the advantages we have.'

Razor nodded, not so much to signal his agreement as to accept that there was no point in challenging his host's version of Guatemalan reality. This was going to be one of those jobs which couldn't end too soon. 'So what exactly do you have in mind?' he asked.

Serrano smiled. 'Well, first, I would like to play you a tape of the man who claims to be El Espíritu.'

He got up and walked across to the expensive sound system in the corner, turned it on, and depressed the play button on the cassette deck.

A calm, philosophical voice floated across the room. The man was asking a series of questions in Spanish, with little clicks in between them to indicate where the answers had been edited out. In the background Chris could hear the faint chirp of a bird. It sounded like a great kiskadee.

Razor listened, conscious that the three Guatemalans were watching him closely. The voice might well belong to the man from Tikal: it held that same distinctive blend of humour and great sadness which he remembered. It probably was him. But Razor didn't feel like betting anyone's life on it.

'It could be,' he admitted. He shrugged. 'Fifteen years is a long time to remember a voice.'

Serrano sat down again. He didn't seem disappointed. 'Easier to remember a face,' he agreed. 'And that is what we hope to arrange.'

'How exactly?' Razor asked.

'We are mounting a surgical operation. A company from Colonel Cabrera's Kaibil Battalion . . . you may have heard of them – they are our special forces. They are on stand-by in Uspantan, in Quiche province, close to the scene of the latest outrage. When we receive the necessary intelligence, which should be within the next few days, the Kaibiles will be going in to pluck out this terrorist gang, and we are hoping you will go along for the ride, as the Americans say. If you are on the spot there will be less chance of mistaken identity, and less time wasted. Yes?'

It was more or less what the SAS men had been expecting. 'You understand that while we are in your country we have to act under specific "rules of engagement",' Razor said. 'We can only use our own weapons in self-defence. We cannot actively assist your troops, even in a matter of law enforcement.'

'Understood,' Serrano agreed.

'But we will expect to be issued with the necessary weapons of self-defence,' Razor persisted, determined to leave no doubts in the man's mind.

'Of course. You have your handguns – your regiment uses Browning High Powers, I believe – and we can supply you with Uzis and whatever else you consider appropriate. That can all be dealt with in Uspantan. I suggest Wednesday morning for the flight – that will give you two whole days to recover from your journey yesterday, and to see some of the city. Lieutenant Gómez has some plans for you, I know.'

'Sounds fine,' Razor said, getting to his feet. He had a strong urge to remove himself from the lounge, the villa, and probably the country as well. Colonel Serrano's expectations sounded reasonable enough, but then the German generals had thought much the same of Hitler's, at least in the beginning. Razor had only finished rereading *The Rommel Papers* a month or so before, and was more sensitive than usual to the perils of soldiers wearing political blinkers.

Serrano seemed content enough, and gave each Englishman a friendly pat on the shoulder as Gómez shepherded them back out to the limousine. Cabrera, who had not uttered a single word since the initial greetings, shook their hands again, as if to seal a non-existent relationship.

In the Pan-American Hotel Hajrija awoke to find Razor already gone. She felt slightly bilious, but nothing worse, and once again thanked her lucky stars that so far she had been spared the horrors of acute morning sickness.

In the shower she found herself smiling at the memory of their lovemaking the night before. The two of them were so good together, and at first she had assumed that he was simply a wonderful lover. Certainly her other experiences in bed had not been half as satisfying. But according to him, neither had his. It seemed that they were only wonderful for each other.

She supposed Razor would be happy when she eventually told him about the baby. For two months now they had been letting nature take its course – not so much trying for a baby as making no effort to prevent one. Abandoning the idea of a defensive midfield anchor in front of the back four, as Razor had so poetically put it.

Her pregnancy had been confirmed on the day he had gone to Birmingham, and the mission had been agreed on before she had had a proper chance to tell him. She had waited several days for a suitable moment before realizing that one was unlikely to appear before this business was over. She knew he was less than enthusiastic about this particular job, and she had no intention of giving him something else to worry about. If she had thought for a moment that the news would make him more careful, then she would have told him. But he was a happy man these days, and in Hajrija's experience happy men – or at least those over thirty – tended not to throw their lives away.

He wasn't the only one who was happy, she thought, smiling at herself as she checked her make-up in the mirror. After the horrors of the war in her country she supposed anything would have looked pretty good, but the two years in England had been more than just a relative blessing. She had picked up her journalistic studies once more, and through a series of articles had built up a reputation as a freelance expert on the affairs of her homeland. She had made friends, both among English people and members of the expatriate Bosnian community. She had a husband whom she loved and who loved her, and a baby on the way. It was all a far cry from waking up to the sound of falling shells, and wondering not only whether she would live to see another day, but whether she really cared one way or the other.

In England she had rarely felt homesick for Bosnia, and it seemed strange that the feeling should have been so strong on her first evening in Guatemala. It might have something to do with being pregnant, she thought, as the grinning bellboy took her down in the hotel lift, but on further reflection she doubted it. There had been something about the Plaza Mayor which had evoked her own country, something beyond the superficial Third World similarities. A feeling of warmth, perhaps. Or community. The word 'solidarity' crossed her mind, like an echo from the Yugoslav past. All these words were clichés. None of them offered an adequate expression of what she had felt.

In the empty dining room she pursued the thought, eating her way through a large plateful of fresh fruit and slowly sipping a cup of milky coffee. It had to have something to do with belief, she decided. Not in God so much as in some sort of wider purpose. Some connectedness. Or something. She suddenly felt determined that the child growing inside her should know other worlds than the ever-so-practical world of the English, who only seemed to indulge their sense of wonder in gardening gloves. Or, in her husband's case, in watching Jürgen Klinsmann.

She smiled to herself, finished the coffee and checked her watch. Razor had said he would either call or return by one o'clock, which left her more than two hours to explore. The guidebook said the area was generally safe in daylight, though not apparently for women on their own. But it probably hadn't been written with female veterans of the Bosnian Army's elite Anti-Sniper Unit in mind. Either way, the Plaza Mayor was bound to be safe.

She left the hotel and retraced their steps of the day before, emerging into the square opposite the flat bulk of the Palacio National. The sky was blue, the sun shining, but there were far fewer people about, and nearly all of them were Ladinos. The Indians were presumably back on their farms, or back in the houses where they lived as servants. Those groups of enchanting young girls with their beautiful woven blouses and skirts and mischievous smiles might even be in school.

Hajrija wandered around the square, not feeling in the slightest bit threatened, but experiencing an absurdly acute sense of loss. There was nothing here to evoke the homeland she loved. On the contrary, the vacant expressions on the faces of the adolescent soldiers were all too reminiscent of that homeland she had been only too glad to escape.

Back in the villa, Serrano poured Cabrera a shot of *aguardiente* and put another cassette in the tape deck. He had already heard the new tape but the Kaibil commander had not. And unlike Serrano, he had personal connections with the Morales family.

The two men listened to the now-familiar voice of the man who called himself El Espíritu, the quiet intensity of the questions and the nightmarish passivity of the answers, the obligatory propaganda, the echoing shot.

'If I ever get my hands on that fucker . . .' Cabrera said emotionally.

'With any luck you will,' Serrano told him. 'Now what did you think of the two Englishmen?'

Cabrera shrugged. 'I expect they are good at what they do.'

'But not much class, eh?'

'They are not officers,' Cabrera said, as if that decided the matter once and for all.

'A good thing too,' Serrano said, pulling the packet of Marlboro Lights from his left breast pocket. 'Officers would be more likely to worry about the whys; these two will just get on with the job.' He flicked the Zippo lighter open. 'Though I did detect some hostility from the younger one.' He smiled wryly. 'But then he's been here for several weeks.'

'Let him be hostile,' Cabrera said. 'The older one made it clear that they don't want to be considered combat personnel, which suits me fine. The realities of our war might be too much for their sensitive stomachs.' He smiled. 'We'll find this bastard, get them to identify him, and then send them home with some souvenirs.'

'OK,' Serrano agreed, 'but as long as they're with you, you'll have to keep a tight rein on your boys – we don't want to solve one PR problem by creating another . . .'

'You want results, don't you?'

'Of course I want results,' Serrano said coldly, 'and I don't expect your Kaibiles to behave like mother's boys. But nothing too gratuitous, not this time. If you want to make examples then wait until after the Englishmen have gone.'

The limousine had just passed under the now-familiar railway bridge and entered the narrower streets of Zona 1. 'How far are we from the hotel?' Razor asked Gómez.

'About two kilometres, perhaps,' the lieutenant said, surprised.

'We'll walk from here. Get some exercise. It's straight down this road, right?'

'But . . .'

'We'll meet you back at the hotel, OK?' Razor tapped the driver on the shoulder and told him in Spanish to stop the car. The driver looked at Gómez, who nodded.

'This area is not a hundred per cent safe,' Gómez said, but Razor and Chris were already climbing out.

'We can probably take care of ourselves,' Razor told him with a grin, and closed the door. The limousine drew away slowly, as if it were dragging the weight of Gómez's reluctance.

On both sides of the street locals were staring at the two men in their strange uniforms.

'They can't wait to get their hands on our berets,' Razor guessed.

'Who could?' Chris agreed, as the two men started ploughing a furrow up the pavement. 'I take it your sudden desire for exercise was a polite fiction.'

'It was claustrophobia. Lieutenant Gómez seems a nice enough lad, but I don't think I'm ever going to feel we're seeing too little of each other. And it'll probably be a damn sight easier to get some time alone here in the city than it will in the great Guatemalan outdoors.'

'And it's harder to bug a street than a limousine or a hotel room,' Chris observed.

'True. Now what did you make of Sooty and Sweep back there?'

Chris grimaced. 'I'll lay you odds Sooty's from G-2. Sweep just seemed like your average Ladino army officer – not very bright, probably a sadist . . .'

'Didn't you like him?'

'What was there to like?'

Razor grinned. 'Well, I guess we're not here to judge a Mr Human Rights contest. They did have their story off pat – one renegade guerrilla putting the peace at risk. And it could be true. According to the FO the negotiations between the Government and the guerrillas are at a crucial stage.'

Chris was silent for a few moments, as they weaved their way through the traffic on 14 Calle. 'I don't know,' he said, as they regained the safety of the pavement, 'maybe the Government wants to kill this guy because he's the strongest card in the guerrillas' hands. They're not going to tell us that, are they? They know we'd much rather believe we're helping a peace process than simply targeting one of their enemies. I mean, fuck it, if I lived in this country I'm not at all sure which side I'd be on. It sure as hell wouldn't be an easy decision.'

Razor sighed. He realized he had been hoping that the job would look more straightforward from close up, not less.

They found Lieutenant Gómez chatting happily with Hajrija at one of the tables in the hotel's covered courtyard. She had already accepted his invitation to take an afternoon tour of the city's sights, and after their hasty departure from the limousine Razor and Chris hadn't the heart to object. And in any case, what else did they have to do?

The limo's first port of call was Minerva Park, and the famous relief map which Ben Manley had mentioned. The horizontal scale was 1:10,000, which reduced Guatemala to the size of a square some fifty metres across. The vertical scale, however, was 1:2000, which exaggerated the mountainous nature of the terrain to an almost ludicrous degree. A *Lord of the Rings* landscape, Razor thought, staring down from one of the two observation towers, and remembering his thoughts of the night before. He asked Gómez to point out the town of Uspantan, and discovered that it was about a hundred kilometres north of the capital, nestling beneath the eastern end of a knife-edged range of mountains called the Cuchumatanes.

Gómez then took them to lunch. The steak-house didn't look much from the outside, but their reception within was almost ecstatic, and the food turned out to be excellent. 'This is the restaurant of my wife's family,' the lieutenant explained, after the owner had insisted on shaking all their hands.

After lunch Gómez suggested the zoo, but was overruled in favour of a drive out of the city. Chris wanted a clearer view of the mountains and volcanoes which rimmed the city, but which only ever appeared peeking above roofs or framed between distant buildings. In addition, Razor was becoming uncomfortably aware of the looks the blacked-out limousine was attracting. Everywhere they went people would catch sight of it and falter in their stride, waiting for the relief of knowing that it had not come for them.

The outskirts of the city proved uglier than the centre. The buildings grew less prosperous, a matter of breeze-blocks and corrugated iron, with rusty steel rods poking optimistically through their roofs. The wide highways were choked with traffic, and to judge from the look and smell of the air, any concern over car emissions had yet to reach Guatemala. Bus after crowded bus went by, each pursued by the black cloud of its own exhaust.

And then suddenly the limousine was pulling out across a wide bridge over a deep ravine, and they could see the city stretching away across the plateau behind them. Ahead of them a land of mountains and valleys receded into the distance, but for the moment their eyes were drawn down into the ravine, where another city, this one arranged in ragged rows of tumbledown shacks, clung to the steep slopes. There was rubbish everywhere, and a smell wafting up from the depths which seemed composed of equal parts of sewage and rotting vegetation.

'Too many people come to the city,' Gómez explained. 'There is no room for them all. But they will not go back to their villages.'

'Why not?' Chris asked.

Gómez shrugged. 'Who knows? I think they expect a miracle.'

They drove another ten kilometres down the Pan-American Highway, before using one of the observation point lay-bys to turn around. The countryside was certainly beautiful, but it was hard to shake the visual memory of the city in the ravine. Even Gómez seemed slightly subdued, though he seemed fully recovered by the time they got back to the hotel. It was now five o'clock, and he cheerfully insisted on their all eating dinner that evening at his home. Razor declined, pleading tiredness, but both Gómez and Hajrija looked so disappointed that he suggested the following evening instead. This proposal was greeted with a huge smile from the lieutenant. He would collect them at six the following evening, though of course he would be checking with them again before then.

When he was gone, Hajrija turned on Razor with an air of amused exasperation. 'What's wrong with you English?' she demanded. 'Don't you like meeting people?'

The three of them ate in the hotel restaurant that evening, at one end of a table laid for about twenty. Without any conscious decision being made, they avoided talking about either Guatemala or the job the two men were about to embark on. Chris asked the others if they had heard from Jamie Docherty, and Hajrija told him about the recent postcard from Chile. 'The beach at Valparaiso,' she said. 'It looked just like the Mediterranean. He said things were going well, but there weren't any details. Isabel has a job with a publisher, but we don't know what he's doing, if anything.'

'Maybe he's writing his memoirs,' Razor suggested.

'If he isn't he should be,' Chris said.

'I could play myself in the movie,' Razor decided.

'We all could,' Chris agreed.

She looked at them both with amusement, then suddenly remembered something. 'I had a letter from Nena,' she told Chris. 'Nothing's changed in Zavik. Which I suppose is good news.'

Chris grunted his agreement. When the three of them had left the Bosnian mountain town with Docherty, Damien Robson (the 'Dame'), six wounded children and one wounded old man, Hajrija's friend Nena had stayed behind, along with her estranged husband Reeve and their two children. In the meantime the town had obviously managed to sustain itself as an oasis of peace in a desert of ethnic madness.

'Another beer?' Razor asked the other two. Remembering those weeks, and the months that had followed, he still sometimes felt like pinching himself. He had journeyed into the horror of Bosnia's war and come back to England happier than he had ever been in his life, a metamorphosis whose only price tag had been several months of recurrent nightmares. According to the SAS shrink they had been his way of expressing the guilt that survivors of tragedies often felt, a questioning of one's right to the life and happiness which so many others had been denied.

And this was the first time the three of them had been

outside England together since those days, Razor realized, as the waiter finally noticed his outstretched arm. Maybe that was one reason for the uneasiness he was feeling. Maybe Guatemala was as innocent as Disneyland.

'A penny for 'em,' Chris said, looking at him.

'He's probably thinking about Tottenham,' Hajrija said crushingly.

'Christ!' Razor exploded, 'I still don't know what happened yesterday.' He pushed back his seat and stood up. 'Order the beers. I'll be back in a minute,' he said.

'Where are you going?' Hajrija shouted after him, but he had already disappeared through the doorway which led to the lobby.

'He's gone to ring the Embassy,' Chris told her.

'The British Embassy will have the football results?'

'Someone there will have heard them on the World Service.'

'The World Service,' she echoed. 'You know, we used to listen to that in Sarajevo, when we were on sniper watch. It was kind of strange, listening to Dave Lee Travis while you waited for a clear shot.'

Chris looked at her. It was sometimes hard to believe that Razor's wife was the same person as the young combat veteran he and Docherty had first met in a seedy hotel near Sarajevo station. He suddenly had an idea. 'What are you going to do when we head up-country?' he asked.

'Do some travelling around, I guess.'

'Well, why don't you spend some time with my family in Antigua – I mean the people I've been staying with. I was booked in until this Saturday, so I doubt they'll have found anyone else. I can call them and ask.'

She thought about it for a second, and then nodded.

'And if you two aren't back by the weekend I can go on to Panajachel. That's where . . .'

A whoop in the distance interrupted her.

'They won,' Chris said unnecessarily.

The following morning Lieutenant Gómez arrived while they were having breakfast. Their departure for Uspantan was still scheduled for early the next day, and his family was excited at the prospect of meeting them all that evening. He approved of Hajrija's plan to stay in Antigua for a few days – 'It is much safer for a woman alone there than here,' he said apologetically – and didn't seem offended when they declined his offer of another day in the limousine. He had one cup of coffee and left again, promising to pick them up at six o'clock.

Chris announced his intention of going off in search of the Botanical Garden, partly out of a genuine desire to see it, and partly because he sensed that the other two would like to spend at least some of their last free day with no more than each other for company. He returned in time to take a shower before meeting Gómez in the entrance, and the two of them waited fifteen minutes for the others to come down.

'Sorry,' Razor said, when they finally did so. 'Our siesta got out of hand,' he added mysteriously.

Gómez didn't seem to notice – he was too busy keeping up a non-stop flow of nervous conversation. This evening was important to him, the two Englishmen belatedly realized.

Instead of the limousine, Gómez had his own Toyota waiting outside. He drove well enough, though his habit of looking over his shoulder to converse with those in the back was somewhat alarming. After about twenty minutes they pulled into the parking lot of a modern-looking apartment block.

They were in Zona 10, Chris noted from a street sign, a step down from the luxury of Zona 14, but several steps up from just about anywhere else.

The apartment itself was clean, tidy and decorated throughout in a safe modern style. Lita Gómez was an attractive Ladina with a mass of dark curls, dark eyes, full mouth and a body teetering on the edge of plumpness. She wore a bright-green dress, high-heeled shoes of the same colour, and large gold earrings. Her English wasn't as good as her husband's, but good enough to make herself understood. At first she also seemed nervous, but her natural ebullience quickly won out, and within ten minutes she and Hajrija were talking like long-lost friends.

The two boys, one ten and the other eight, were obviously miffed at having to miss watching TV, but they nevertheless joined in the conversation with their father and the two SAS men, and in the process displayed a patience and politeness which many an English parent would have died for. Both wanted to be soldiers when they grew up, a fact which obviously both pleased and worried their father. Razor found himself liking the man more in his home than he had in the limousine.

The dinner was delicious, but seemed little more Guatemalan than the décor. The conversation moved easily enough from travel to TV, fashion to music, food to sports. Lita was enthralled by the story of how Razor and Hajrija had met, and her husband, to Chris's complete surprise, turned out to have a library of books on bird-watching almost as large as his own. The two boys insisted on showing Razor their collection of World Cup bubblegum cards. The thorny subject of politics surfaced only once, and then only in connection with President Clinton's abortive attempt to end the American baseball strike.

All in all it was a thoroughly enjoyable evening, and leaving the brightly lit family apartment for the dark and vaguely sinister streets of the city felt almost traumatic. Sitting in the back of the Toyota with Hajrija, Razor had a picture of a society living in rigid, self-contained compartments. As long as you stayed in your compartment, he thought, then things could be OK. The Ladinos, or at least some of them, had their wealth and their dreams of an American consumerist world. The Indians had something else, something which he didn't suppose he would ever understand. And whether or not that something made up, or more than made up, for their downtrodden situation he couldn't begin to know.

The problem was the compartments themselves. Ricardo Gómez and El Espíritu might both be reasonable human beings in their own little spaces, but that was only half the story. When people lived in such ignorance of each other, then opening doors became a dangerous business. In such situations the first reaction was usually shock, and the second was often cruelty.

Razor thought about Gómez sitting in the driver's seat in front of him, and caught him smiling in the rear-view mirror, presumably with pleasure at how well the evening had gone. Earlier he had watched him reading bedtime stories to his two boys, and noted how much enjoyment all three had derived from this simple ritual.

Once in the mountains, Razor asked himself, would this Gómez and his comrades all metamorphose into something else, Guatemalan Jekylls into Hydes, family men into the torturers for which their army was notorious?

5

There was a brisk rap on the door. '*Es cuarto para las dos*,' a voice said softly.

'OK,' Razor half shouted in reply, and groaned as the footsteps outside receded. 'Shit, I'm getting too old for this,' he muttered.

'Another day in paradise,' Chris said from the bunk above.

Their small barracks room was far from pitch-dark: the faintest of natural lights was seeping in through the small window and a brighter electric glow was outlining the ill-fitting door.

'If they've got the lights on out there, we might as well have ours on in here,' Chris said, lowering himself to the floor and reaching for the switch.

The two men, both already dressed in their jungle combat fatigues, sat side by side on the lower bunk lacing up their boots, and then took turns with the small hand mirror and make-up kit.

'I must have been a beautician in an earlier life,' Razor remarked, admiring his own handiwork.

'Frankenstein's, I should think.'

Razor laughed, and ran one last check on the Mini-Uzi 9mm sub-machine-gun. The SAS did not normally carry

Uzis, but the gun's worldwide popularity with terrorists and counter-terrorists alike had made familiarization a necessary part of their training. Razor didn't find the Uzi as user-friendly as the Heckler & Koch MP5, but there was no doubting its simple reliability. And with any luck, this time around he wouldn't have to do anything other than carry it.

It was one minute to two. 'Ready?' he asked Chris, who nodded. The two men pulled the unusually lightweight bergens over their shoulders, donned their floppy jungle camouflage hats, and let themselves out into the corridor.

The eighty-strong assault company of Kaibiles had already evacuated the barracks, which Razor supposed was a good sign. He had watched them do their physical training on the base's football pitch the previous afternoon and been provisionally impressed. They were fit, and they looked tough, not to say downright mean. They had the weapons – Uzis, recoilless rifles, mortars – and tactical air support when it was needed. Whether they could fight was something else.

It was considerably darker outside, though no obvious attempt was being made to conceal their departure from any watchers in either the nearby town or the surrounding hills. Maybe Colonel Cabrera had decided that the sound of the trucks would be enough in itself to torpedo any hopes of the company sneaking away unobserved. Maybe he was right.

Lieutenant Gómez, his smile a little more nervous than usual, was waiting to guide them into the second of the four trucks. The SAS men squeezed in beside the grinning Kaibiles, and a few moments later the driver put the truck in gear and pulled slowly away, passing under the sentry tower which loomed above the gate and rolling down the road towards the town. Through the open back of the truck they could see the bright headlights of the two following vehicles and the faint silhouette of the sentry tower against a moonless sky.

The trucks rumbled down Uspantan's cobbled streets, and swung left around the square, past the pale cathedral and up another steep street of silent houses. There was a brief glimpse of cornfields clinging to steep valley sides before a forest engulfed the road in darkness. Two hours, Cabrera had told them. Razor sat back and closed his eyes.

They had left Guatemala City soon after eight on the morning of the previous day. The Chinook CH-47D had lifted off from the military side of Aurora Airport, rising up through thick mist to reveal the flat crest of a distant volcano floating serenely on the layer of low cloud, and then headed north across a landscape of hills and valleys which seemed to have been first modelled in papier mâché, then draped in earth and trees. Mist swirled in the valley bottoms, and verdant mountains rose in the distance through layers of fluffy white cloud. Ribbons of winding road connected small towns, each of them laid out on the familiar grid pattern, each with a shining white church at its centre. Uspantan had been the last of these, and the Chinook had flown low over the central square before touching down at the base above the town.

Colonel Cabrera had been there to meet them, along with his number two, whom he introduced as Major Romeo Valdez Osorio. The major was clean-shaven, and as fair-skinned for a Guatemalan Hispanic as the colonel was dark. He had wavy, chestnut-brown hair, serious blue eyes, and seemed to be in his early thirties. His hands, Razor noticed, were beautifully manicured. His greeting had been polite but guarded.

Cabrera had seemed a different proposition from the man they had met in Serrano's villa. Perhaps he had found those circumstances inhibiting, because here, back in his natural habitat, he was all wide smiles and expansive gestures, and full of enthusiasm for the job in hand. At the dinner table he and the other officers had plied the two SAS men with questions about the Falklands War, a subject in which they were surprisingly well versed. They had little sympathy for their Latin American comrades-in-arms – as one officer put it: 'The Argentines should stick to football.'

Now, sitting in the heaving truck, Razor wondered where Cabrera and Osorio were. Probably in the truck's cab, he guessed. It had to be more comfortable than the back.

Any trace of a paved road had long since vanished, and every now and then the rear wheels would live up to their name, rearing up like the proverbial bucking bronco, and crashing the company back down on their tail-bones with jarring effect. Bloody torture, Razor thought, and smiled grimly to himself in the dark. That was probably not a diplomatic phrase to use in this part of the world.

Next to him Chris seemed to be sleeping through it all, which had to rate as some kind of miracle. Razor thought about his wife, who would soon be starting her second day in Antigua, and wished to God he was there with her.

The journey ground on, the trucks fighting their way up the dirt track into the Cuchumatanes. It was a quarter to four when they reached their destination, and disgorged the troops on to the road. Jumping down gratefully, the two Englishmen found themselves surrounded by dense forest, and a silence broken only by the shuffling of human feet.

The only light came from the starfields twinkling above the canopy of trees.

Ten metres away they could see Cabrera and Osorio examining a map by torchlight with a small man in civilian clothes. As if aware of their eyes on him, the man glanced in their direction, and they could see his Indian features reflected in the yellow light. His expression seemed almost unnaturally neutral, as if life had burned the emotion out of him.

Razor found himself thinking about all the Westerns he had watched as a kid. The Indian scout who helped the white men had usually come to a bad end.

The first of the Kaibiles filed off down an invisible path. Gómez inserted himself and the two Englishmen somewhere in the middle of the departing column, and for the next hour and a half they trekked up and down hills, through trees and across bare slopes, seeing little more than the man directly in front of them. Razor was impressed by the disciplined silence of the Guatemalan soldiers, and by how at home they seemed in the wilderness. Whatever else the Kaibiles might be, they were not parade-ground soldiers.

There was still no sign of light in the eastern sky when the column arrived at the location selected for the ambush. The SAS men had been shown a small-scale map of the immediate area – a thickly wooded narrow valley which carried a path allegedly used by the guerrillas – but for the moment they had to take the geography on trust. Along with Gómez they were allocated to the reserve platoon, which was under orders to seek concealment high on the valley side, some fifty metres above the units charged with initially engaging the enemy. Whether this was to keep them out of harm's way or to prevent them from witnessing any over-exuberance on the part of the Kaibiles, it was impossible to say. Maybe a bit of both.

The soldiers in the reserve platoon were soon at work digging themselves in, and Razor could imagine the surprised looks he and Chris were getting, as they sat there with their backs against a tree. Eventually Gómez could restrain himself no longer. 'We must dig too,' he said. 'If you like, I do all the digging.'

'We'll dig our own scrape,' Razor told him. 'When there's enough light to choose the best spot.'

'Ah, I see,' Gómez said, and sat down again.

Razor smiled at him absent-mindedly, his mind going back to the last time he had encountered this problem, on a snow-covered slope above the Serb-held village of Vogosca. He and Hajrija – who had then been no more than a beautiful dream – had been ordered to establish a forward observation post above the town. They had spent the last fifteen minutes of darkness cutting tiles of frozen snow for roofing over the yet-to-be-located hide. There was no snow here, but it was cold enough now that they had stopped walking. Ten minutes later the sky was showing its first hint of light, and over the next twenty minutes the two men watched the valley slowly swim into focus. It was only about fifty metres wide at the bottom, and in several places the trees grew right down to the edge of the stream. There were two clearings, both apparently man-made. The larger one, though now overgrown with weeds, had once been cultivated; the smaller contained the ruins of what must have been the cultivator's shack. From what they could see the path seemed to wind down from the narrow pass some three hundred metres to their left and then hug the side of the stream as it descended the valley.

Cabrera would presumably have his forward units on two sides of the larger clearing, deployed to catch the guerrillas in a lethal crossfire without risk to themselves.

When they were satisfied as to the best point for observation, Razor and Chris swiftly dug out a simple scrape in the shelter of a large bush, covered it with the rain ponchos from their bergens, and added a few pieces of foliage for artistic effect. Once ensconced, they tossed a coin for first watch, and Razor won. Despite the cold and damp he was asleep almost immediately.

Chris took out his binoculars and conducted a more thorough investigation of the terrain above and below them. The Kaibil platoons were hidden in the expected places, but well hidden nevertheless. If the guerrillas came down that path, as they were presumably expected to do, there would certainly be a few bodies for Razor to examine.

Chris turned his field-glasses up the valley to where the path climbed over the pass, almost dreading the thought of catching the approach of distant figures. But there were no humans in sight, only a single large bird – a black vulture, he thought – lazily circling in the air currents above the pass. Anticipating carrion, perhaps.

The day swiftly brightened, and as the sun burned off the clouds the landscape assumed that high-altitude clarity which Chris had first known and loved in the Colombian Andes. It would be a gorgeous day for hiking, he thought, fixing the binoculars on the distant snow-covered peaks which now lay framed in the 'V' of the pass to his left. Unless you were a guerrilla, of course, in which case such clarity could easily prove fatal. They would be much more likely to move by night, Chris thought.

So what made Cabrera expect otherwise? Information

received, no doubt. But received how? If force had been used then the information was probably worthless.

'Whatever,' Chris murmured to himself, just as a bird started singing 'pur-wheee' somewhere close by. He started searching with the binoculars for the unknown vocalist, and soon found it – a small bird crouching on a branch some twenty metres away. As he watched, the bird suddenly leapt into flight, displaying white patches in blunt-tipped wings. Chris jotted down the particulars in his notebook and reached into the bergen for his well-thumbed copy of *Birds of Costa Rica*, wishing someone would hurry up and produce a volume for Guatemala. After a short search he found the bird – a pauraque.

Over the next couple of hours he saw and heard several more of them, albeit with diminishing frequency. The presence of so many humans, no matter how silent their presence, was gradually scaring the birds away. The guerrillas might have reasons for marching in broad daylight, Chris thought, but even the most basic nature awareness would alert them to the unnaturalness of the silence which now pervaded this particular valley.

The morning wore on, and at noon a yawning Razor took charge of the binoculars. For the next ten minutes or so he swept the valley and its surrounds, and reached the same conclusion as his partner – for this ambush to prove successful the guerrillas would need to demonstrate incompetence above and beyond the expected. And nothing in Razor's recollections of El Espíritu suggested any such level of stupidity.

So today was unlikely to see an end of it. In fact the whole business could drag on for weeks, which wasn't a very appealing prospect. 'Join the Army and stare at the same line of trees for eight hours on end,' he said to himself.

For the next few hours he alternated keeping watch through the binoculars with playing one of his favourite mental games, which involved remembering the plots of famous Hollywood films and then bringing them up to date. Jamie Docherty had invented the game, and there was no doubting its efficiency when it came to consuming stretches of otherwise dead time. Razor spent much of the afternoon recalling the twists and turns of *Casablanca* before trying, unsuccessfully, to relocate the action in a modern context. Bogart, Bergman and her unbearable goody-goody husband were easy enough, but police chief Louis was a real problem. Razor couldn't find a current equivalent of the semi-independent Vichy regime in Morocco, and the more he thought about it the more crucial the balance of power between Louis and his Nazi colleague was to the plot. Without it everything else fell apart.

'Here's looking at you, kid,' he murmured, and picked up the binoculars again. He checked the pass, shifted his sights along the opposite side of the valley, and found a guerrilla looking at him through a similar pair of long-distance lenses.

The man was dressed in olive-green fatigues and a matching baseball cap. He stared at Razor for a few seconds, then took the glasses away from his eyes, and seemed almost to smile before disappearing abruptly into the foliage. Razor tried to find him again, but failed, and almost began to wonder if he had imagined the sighting.

So much for the ambush, he thought. The next question was whether to report what he had just seen. If he did, he would be actively interfering in someone else's war, and probably condemning the smiling guerrilla to death and worse. If he didn't, he could hardly be accused of helping the guerrillas to evade the ambush – they had obviously managed that much on their own.

Unless he saw any sign that the guerrillas were planning their own ambush, Razor decided, he would let the Kaibiles find their own targets.

Some four hundred metres to the north-west, just behind the ridge which separated the site of the intended ambush from the next valley, Tomás was running through the trees, listening for sounds of the chase that must be underway. There was no doubting that the soldier had seen him: Tomás had been wondering who the man was, and had probably kept the glasses on him for too long, creating that sixth-sense awareness of being watched which had led to his own discovery.

The man was probably an American or an Israeli, though he had hardly seemed big enough for one of the former, and much too pale-skinned for one of the latter. Not that it mattered who the bastard was – no gringos who sold their services to the Kaibiles could expect any mercy from the *compas*.

A minute passed, and Tomás could still detect no signs of a pursuit above the sounds of his own passage. He risked halting his flight for a few seconds, crouching down beside a tree and listening intently while he recovered his breath. There was nothing – no sounds of running feet, no shouts, no baying dogs, no distant drone of helicopters. It was as if the foreigner with the field-glasses had dropped dead with shock at the sight of him.

Tomás started running again, hardly daring to believe his own luck.

When Razor woke Chris at six the sun was almost gone, the valley below already shrouded in darkness. Lieutenant Gómez's presence made it impossible for Razor to share the news of his sighting with his SAS partner, but that didn't seem too much of a problem. He had seen no signs of searchlights among the Kaibiles' equipment, and assumed they would soon receive word that Cabrera was calling it a day. And a pretty futile one at that.

Another half an hour went by, drawing the night down across the sky. Razor was just wondering how to find out what the hell the Kaibil CO was doing when a scream sounded across the valley, pulling silence after it like a shroud.

'What the fuck?' Chris growled.

In the darkness the voices of the nearby Kaibiles were animated, almost exultant.

Another scream rang out, quieter this time, almost animal-like. Maybe it was an animal. Maybe . . .

A single shot resounded.

'Ricardo,' Razor said coldly. 'What the fuck's going on down there?'

Gómez spread his hands. 'I do not know,' he replied.

'I think we ought to find out,' Razor said, getting to his feet and staring down into the murk of the valley.

'No, I will go,' Gómez said, a pleading tone in his voice.

Razor looked at him, and then at Chris. 'OK,' he agreed.

The liaison officer disappeared down the slope.

'I wish to God we had a nightscope,' Razor muttered.

'We might not like what we see,' Chris said.

'No.'

They had been waiting almost a quarter of an hour when Gómez reappeared. 'We are returning to the base at Uspantan,' he said, as if that answered all their questions.

'And the screaming and the shot?'

'Oh, one of the men walked into a snake that was hanging from a branch. He panicked, but his comrade shot the snake.' Gómez spewed out the words in a rush, as if eager to get rid of them. And even in the darkness it was obvious that he was strenuously avoiding eye contact.

Two hours later, as they waited on the road for the trucks to return and collect the company, the two Englishmen looked in vain for any sign of the Indian guide.

Hajrija watched Maria Martínez stir three sugars into her coffee and wondered how the girl managed to keep her figure. It was partly sheer youth, she supposed, and partly the non-stop outpouring of nervous energy. Maria was presumably working on the theory that the more she said the more Hajrija would understand, because she had hardly stopped talking in the two hours they had been out together. She was talking now.

'*Más despacio*,' Hajrija told her. More slowly.

Maria grinned and tried again, mixing in some mime for good measure. Eventually Hajrija understood that she was talking about the ruined nunnery which they had just visited, and the small cells where particularly devout nuns had permanently incarcerated themselves, all the better to realize the glory of God.

'All the life,' Maria added indignantly in English, as if the nuns had done it just to spite her. 'No music, no dancing, no sex,' she said, picking up the chocolate croissant. 'No life,' she concluded, biting into it.

Hajrija smiled. It was hard for her to sympathize with the nuns' self-denial, even when it was being attacked in the name of self-indulgence. Looking at the convent cells, her first thought had been of lives without children.

She wished now she had told Razor about the baby.

He woke up in the barracks room shortly after seven in the morning, and reached out lazily for a wife who wasn't there. He groaned inwardly and lay there for a while, mulling over the difficult situation he and Chris were in. No clever means of extrication occurred to him.

The trucks had arrived back at the Uspantan base soon after midnight, and the deflated soldiers had been sent straight to their barracks. Razor and Chris had been invited to a post-mortem with drinks, but on impulse Razor had pleaded tiredness. He knew it would be futile to ask about the Indian guide – would, in fact, simply alienate Cabrera – but he was weary enough not to trust his own sense of discretion, particularly with a drink in his hand. In the morning, he had reasoned, he would probably find it easier to keep a cool head.

And, lying there on the bunk, he supposed he did feel more resigned. The anger was still there, but its focus seemed to have shifted, away from bastards like Cabrera and Osorio, and more towards the bastards in Washington and London who had agreed to help them.

There was a stirring in the bunk above, a groan, and the sudden appearance of the familiar face and spiky hair.

'Just realized where you are?' Razor asked.

'Dead right.'

'I don't know what you're complaining about – governments seem to be queuing up to pay for your bird-watching expeditions these days.'

'Not to mention your family holidays,' Chris retorted.

'Some holiday.'

Chris lowered himself out of the upper bunk and down to the floor. 'So let's go out on the sun terrace and order breakfast.'

'They never have Weetabix at these posh resorts,' Razor said, reaching for his trousers.

A couple of minutes later they were walking across the grassy parade ground, enjoying their first taste of another gorgeous day. The blue sky hung above the amphitheatre of mountains, and the sun lit the white church which rose from the centre of the town below. For the twenty seconds it took to reach the canteen, it was possible to believe that those who lived in Guatemala had been blessed.

Once inside, they were served tortilla, rice and refried beans by a smiling adolescent boy. The meal tasted better than it looked, which wasn't difficult. The accompanying coffee tasted worse, which was.

'And these are the privileged troops,' Chris murmured, just as Gómez spotted them from the doorway. The lieutenant hoped they had slept well, that the breakfast wasn't too bad – a rueful smile, here – and that they would accompany him to the colonel's office.

This was in the small building next door, and looked very much a temporary affair. The Kaibiles, Razor realized, would be shifted around the country to where they were most needed at any given time. Such a *modus operandi* would not only make military sense, but also deeply affect the character of the regiment. The life of eternal nomads would both strengthen the regiment's morale and prevent it from forming any human ties with the people of a particular locality. They were like a praetorian guard, Razor thought, with the families of Zona 14 standing in for an emperor.

Colonel Cabrera was sitting behind his desk, talking to the standing Major Osorio. He greeted the SAS men with a smile, asked the same questions as Gómez concerning their sleep and breakfast, and apologized for what he called 'yesterday's fiasco'. Their source of information had proved untrustworthy.

'So we understood,' Razor said coldly.

Cabrera chose to ignore the tone. 'The next operation will be more successful,' he promised, 'but it may be a couple of days, perhaps more, before we can move again. Is there anything you need or want?'

Razor looked at Chris, who shook his head. 'No thanks. I assume it's safe for us to take a look at the town?'

Cabrera looked surprised for a moment, but quickly recovered. 'Of course. It is perhaps more sensible to visit in the daylight. Uspantan is a safe town, but there are criminals everywhere. In the daylight they hide. And I'm sure Lieutenant Gómez can find you somewhere good to eat lunch.'

Gómez looked doubtful, but agreed nevertheless.

Walking round Uspantan proved a depressing business. The smiles which had characterized each meeting of eyes in Guatemala's Plaza Mayor, and the sense of joy which had been so much a part of that evening, were both conspicuous by their absence. As the three men strolled around the streets only the children offered anything other than a cold stare in response to their greetings. Gómez clearly found it hard to understand, and became both angry and apologetic.

'Don't worry about it,' Razor told him, wondering as he did so at how little Gómez understood of his own country. Uspantan was the Falls Road without the graffiti – sullen, resentful, an occupied town.

The largest hotel was apparently owned by a Ladino, but the only staff on display were Indians. They served up a typical *comida* lunch, which Gómez insisted on paying for. Outside the hotel he hopefully asked the SAS men if they had seen enough.

But Razor had spotted a Guatel office on the other side of the square. 'I'd like to call Hajrija,' he told the liaison officer.

'It will be quicker from the base.'

'Can't we do it from over there?' Razor asked. 'I don't like taking up a military line for a personal call,' he added ingenuously.

Gómez failed to come up with a better reason for refusal. 'Yes, you can call from there,' he agreed.

The three men walked across to the tiny office, and began negotiating with the man in charge. Half an hour and several breakdowns later the man achieved what only twenty minutes earlier he had described as impossible, connecting Razor with the Antigua number which Chris had supplied.

He listened to it ring, inwardly praying that she would be there. She was, and for ten minutes they chatted about nothing in particular, simply happy to hear each other's voice. She was going to Panajachel on the following day, she said, and gave him the name of the hotel at which she was planning to stay. Not trusting the phone, he told her nothing about how their mission was going, save to say that there was no sign of it soon being over.

After hanging up, he paid the operator in quetzals and walked slowly across to where the others were sitting on a bench, feeling surprised, and even a little ashamed, at how much he missed her.

Having spent much of the previous night returning by a deliberately circuitous route to the *compa* camp, Tomás slept through most of the daylight hours. The sun was barely above the horizon when Emelia woke him, and the distant mountains were turning purple in the fading light.

'There's an operations meeting,' Emelia told him.

Tomás rubbed his eyes, yawned, and kicked aside the thin blanket. 'I'm on my way,' he said.

He left her opening the Spanish primer, and walked up to the ancient ruins, where the rest of the *subcomandantes* had already gathered. The large chunks of broken stone had once been part of an ancient fort, from which their ancestors had tried in vain to defy the Spanish invaders. The latter and their descendants had long since forgotten the place, but the Mayan Indians had not, and the continuity which it represented always gave Tomás a feeling of strength. Sometimes he thought he could almost smell the incense which had been burned here half a millennium before.

He found a space in the rough circle and sat down.

'OK, Tomás,' the Old Man said, 'tell the others what you saw yesterday morning.'

'Kaibiles,' Tomás said tersely, looking round at the other seven faces in the circle. 'About company strength – roughly a hundred men. They were concealed in the trees, so I couldn't get an accurate count. Just below the pass, in the valley of the Chitac. You know, the old Jimón farm.' He smiled. 'They were waiting for some guerrillas to march over the pass singing revolutionary songs.'

'I think we know who they were waiting for,' the Old Man said softly.

'Yes,' Alicia agreed, 'but why there?'

'One of our people was with them,' Tomás said. 'I didn't recognize him.'

'Shit,' Gerardo muttered, sounding sad rather than angry. They all knew the many kinds of pressure the Army could exert. 'He probably just took them somewhere that would seem convincing,' he added.

'Maybe,' the Old Man said. 'But the important thing is that the Kaibiles know we are in the area . . .'

'They could be guessing,' someone suggested hopefully.

'They could be, but I doubt it. And there's something else,' he added, looking at Tomás. 'There were two gringos with them.'

'*Norteamericanos*,' Gerardo spat out contemptuously.

'Maybe,' Tomás said. 'One of them could have been a *norteamericano* – he had the short hair that looks like a brush – but the other . . . I don't know. But that is not the important thing. The second man, he saw me – we found each other with our field-glasses at exactly the same moment, and I don't think he can have told anyone. There was no alarm, no one followed me, and when I was sure of that I went back. They were still deployed for the ambush.'

There was a silence while the others took this in.

'Maybe he took you for one of the Kaibiles,' Rosa said at last.

'That is not funny,' Tomás said indignantly.

'But possible,' the Old Man admitted. 'There is no way we can know, so we must leave it as a mystery for the moment. What we need to decide now is where we go from here. And as I see it we have only two choices – retreat or engagement. We cannot just go to ground in this area.'

'But can we take on the Kaibiles?' Alicia asked doubtfully.

'Not on ground of their choosing, no. But on ground that we have chosen – perhaps that could be a different story.' The Old Man let his eyes drift around the circle. 'We knew when we started this that the risks would grow greater with each day that passed.'

6

Soon after ten o'clock on Sunday morning, with the base canteen coffee still rumbling in their stomachs, Razor and Chris climbed into the jeep which Gómez had requisitioned for their trip to Chul, the nearest of the so-called 'model villages'. Two Kaibil soldiers were accompanying them, one at the wheel and one perched precariously on the back.

Gómez had suggested the trip the previous evening, and the SAS men had decided that anything would be better than a whole day spent either sitting round the base or wandering round a hostile town. Razor had also told himself, without much conviction, that it was only fair to see the other side of the argument. If the Army really was doing something positive in the area, that would at least be some compensation for all the rest. And it might make him feel better about being in the position he was in.

Chul was about fifteen kilometres from Uspantan, but the drive, down one broad valley by paved road and up a long and narrow one by dirt track, took the best part of an hour. The village nestled in a flat fold of the foothills of the Cuchumatanes and at first sight looked remarkably like an Alpine village, with neat rows of wooden houses and well-kept fields surrounded by forested slopes. But there was something very un-Guatemalan about it, Chris thought, as the jeep descended the winding approach road. Chul looked more like a model than a real village.

A flat, triangular space with one set of football posts occupied the village centre. While Gómez went looking for the local *comandante*, the two Englishmen wandered out on to the thick grass, gazing around them. The whitewashed church was the only adobe building; all the houses were timber-built, as was the tall and apparently unmanned watch-tower. The streets were unpaved, a mess of mud and pebbles, but new lights had been installed.

The classic Third World sense of priorities, Chris thought. Electricity brought radios and TVs, the lure of the city and a world built around money and the hunger for things. It made the rural areas dependent on the city. A decent water supply and sewage system on the other hand . . . well, they might improve the health of the local people, but they would also encourage a dangerous sense of independence.

There was at least a standpipe in the village. Three women were gathered round it now, chatting with each other as they filled up identical green and white striped plastic jars. They didn't seem bothered by the Kaibiles or the gringos, which Razor and Chris assumed had to be a good sign.

An Army officer emerged from one of the nearby houses, trailing Gómez in his wake. He was young, and wore old-fashioned circular-rimmed glasses which reminded Razor of Julie Christie's husband in *Doctor Zhivago*. There was no fanaticism in this man's eyes, though – only a sort of harassed cheerfulness. He introduced himself as Major Francisco Gramajo, shook their hands, asked the usual question about how they liked Guatemala, and took them on a tour of a building which served as both the medical centre and food distribution outlet. The villagers, he explained, received both medical help and supplies free of charge. All the men had to do in return was spend so much time each week undertaking communal duties, like road repairs, reconstruction and stints with the Civil Patrols.

He then took them on a walk round the village, greeting by name each person who crossed their path. The villagers' response was polite enough, if somewhat lacking in enthusiasm.

'What happened to the old village?' Chris asked him, having glimpsed traces of several former buildings.

'It was burned by the *subversivos*,' Gramajo explained. 'Seven, eight years ago now. The people who lived here ran away, and there was no village here for several years. Then the Government brought in new settlers, and they replanted the land' – he gestured towards the cornfields in the distance – 'and of course the Army was given the primary responsibility for their safety. But not all – the new settlers were only too happy to form Civil Patrols and make certain there was no chance of the *subversivos* returning. And, as you can see, it is working. The villagers here have a good life – enough land, food, medicine.' He glanced at them, as if expecting agreement.

'Looks good,' Razor said diplomatically.

'It is,' Gómez agreed with a satisfied smile.

They went back to Gramajo's office in the Army headquarters building, where a *comida* lunch was waiting, along with half a crate of ice-cold Gallo beer. The Indian women who served them seemed pleasant enough, but there was no disguising the reserve in their eyes. None of the four men sitting at the table had any idea what these women were thinking, Razor thought. Chul seemed benign enough on the surface, but it was another occupied town. And who knew how much of the apparent placidity had been deliberately staged for their benefit. Gómez seemed as innocent of deception as ever, but then it could just as well have been staged for his benefit too.

On the drive back to Uspantan Razor decided that there was no way for a foreigner to be certain of where right and wrong lay in Guatemala – the place was too surreal, too Alice-in-Wonderlandish. In the last resort there was nothing to rely on but his own instincts, and he supposed he should have known that all along.

'Fuck it,' he muttered to himself, and decided to give his brain a rest, at least for the duration of the ride back to the base. Whatever else Guatemala might be, it was certainly beautiful, and he let his eyes feast on the landscape, each shade and line so vibrant in the clear mountain air.

In the adjoining seat, Chris was thinking about his partner while his eyes scanned the trees and sky for birds. He had few doubts concerning their mission in Guatemala – as far as he was concerned, it simply stank of political opportunism. But he was only along for the ride, whereas Razor was actually required to give these people something. Chris could understand why that might involve a degree of wishful thinking. No one wanted to believe they were helping the bad guys.

Having that wishful thinking slowly dissolve was no doubt a painful process – it was certainly painful to watch. But as far as Chris could see there was nothing they could do about their situation, or at least not until Razor got the chance to identify either prisoners or corpses. When that time came he could simply refuse to pick out the man the Guatemalan Army wanted, and at least keep his conscience clear on one account. Of course, a new problem might then arise – the Army could demand their continued presence until such time as Razor did identify someone as El Espíritu.

It was a no-win situation all right. Chris found himself wondering what Jamie Docherty would have done, and decided the Scot would have been just as stuck as they were.

They reached the end of the dirt track and turned west along the paved road, just as a bus rattled through in the opposite direction, trailing the usual toxic cloud of exhaust. They were only a few miles from Uspantan when Chris spotted a turkey vulture hanging almost motionless above the valley. He turned his field-glasses on the bird, which seemed to stare straight back at him before wheeling to match the speed of the jeep, and fly a course almost directly above their own. Chris pointed it out to Razor, who stared up at the vulture with an ironic smile. Its shadow, Chris realized, could be seen on the road ahead, as if they were following in its wake.

On the outskirts of Uspantan the vulture peeled away and headed back down the valley, as if it had successfully completed its task of escorting them through its territory. They drove through the town and up the steep hill to the military base, stopped for the obligatory security check at the gate, and finally pulled up outside the main barracks.

'Siesta time,' Chris suggested, before Gómez could suggest anything else.

'Sounds good . . .' Razor began, but the distant scream cut him off.

It was a muffled scream, but there was no mistaking the

agony which had fuelled it. And as Razor caught Gómez's reluctant eye, it sounded again.

Razor looked down at the ground for a moment, then abruptly turned on his heel and started across the grass in the direction of Colonel Cabrera's office. Chris hurried after him. 'Señor Wilkinson,' Gómez pleaded. 'Señores.'

Reaching the headquarters building, Razor ignored the tentative requests of the duty sentries and walked straight in. He didn't bother to knock on Cabrera's door either, simply swinging it open and marching inside. The colonel and his number two were in almost the same positions – one sitting, one standing – as they had been the day before. Watching Cabrera's face, Razor saw sudden fear give way to anger and anger to an empty smile. 'Señores,' he said brightly, 'what can . . . ?'

'There is someone being tortured on this base,' Razor said flatly.

'That is not . . .' Cabrera started to say, when the faint but unmistakable sound of another scream drifted in through the open door.

'We were assured by your Government,' Razor went on relentlessly, 'that this operation would be conducted with due respect for accepted standards of human rights. We will not be a party to inhumane treatment of prisoners, and I demand that whatever is going on here be stopped immediately.'

Cabrera half rose out of his chair, his face reddening.

Osorio's face had gone white. 'You demand?!' he hissed. 'This is not your country. You . . .'

'Major,' Cabrera said warningly, before Osorio could add anything else. The younger man's anger seemed to have defused his own, or at least given him time to conceal it.

'It is you who asked us for help,' Razor said coldly. He was shaking inside.

'Yes, yes,' Cabrera agreed. 'Please . . . you must understand, this is a war situation, we have to interrogate people, and sometimes . . . well, when their comrades' lives are at stake, then the interrogators get carried away. I am not excusing this, simply trying to explain it. We will attend to the matter. Major,' he said, nodding at Osorio, who gave the two Englishmen one last angry look and stalked out. 'He will see to it,' Cabrera said. 'I apologize for his words. He is a patriot, you understand, and young. He finds it hard to accept direction from outsiders.' Cabrera smiled. 'I'm sure that you would not like Guatemalans telling your English officers how to behave in your Northern Ireland.'

'No,' Razor agreed. He felt certain of Cabrera's insincerity, and no less angry, but there was nothing else to say. 'Thank you, Colonel,' he ground out.

'It is my pleasure.'

The two Englishmen withdrew from the office past an ashen Gómez, and the last thing they heard was Cabrera telling the lieutenant to close the door. 'Maybe he brought us back too soon,' Chris wondered out loud.

Razor said nothing.

They walked back across the parade ground, hearing no screams.

'For all I know, they've just put a sock in the poor bastard's mouth,' Razor said bitterly.

Chris shrugged. 'You couldn't have done any more. If they want to torture someone, it won't be hard to find somewhere out of earshot.'

'Yeah, I know.'

Back in their room the two men stretched out on their

bunks, Razor with his novel, Chris with his Walkman. He started off with U2's *Joshua Tree*, but soon exchanged it for R.E.M.'s *Monster* – some of the lines on the former just seemed a bit too close to home. '*A heart of darkness, a firezone ... his blood still cries from the ground ... where bullets rape the night of the merciful ...*' It was easier to get lost in the sheer exuberance of Peter Buck's power-chords.

The afternoon dragged by, and they went for an early supper in the deserted canteen. It was there that Gómez found them. He greeted them with a smile, but there was distress in his eyes. The world was not working the way it should, with conflict replacing the harmony he loved, and himself caught in the middle. He sat down beside them but didn't say anything for a moment, as if he was building up the courage to do so. 'It is Sunday night,' he said eventually, 'and Colonel Cabrera has told me to ask you if you would like some female company.'

Razor and Chris looked at each other. 'Thank the colonel,' Razor told the Guatemalan, 'but no.'

'I understand,' Gómez said quickly, getting to his feet. 'You have happy marriage.'

'Yeah,' said Razor tersely.

They watched him leave the canteen, both feeling sorry for him.

'This is turning into a fucking mess,' Razor said. 'And the temptation to just pack it in and go home is getting stronger every day.'

Chris looked at him. 'What makes you think they'd let us go?'

* * *

Sixty-five kilometres to the south, Hajrija was sitting in the aptly named Sunset Café, watching the last throes of the day. Across Lake Atitlán the three volcanoes were starkly silhouetted against a deep-red sky, offering a vista which seemed almost too postcard-perfect to be true.

All around, fellow tourists were picking at bowls of nachos and drinking Cuba Libres, cold Gallos, even milk shakes. Between taking snaps they fended off the beautiful little Indian girls who were trying to sell them miniature dolls, parrot necklaces, purses and friendship bracelets. Hajrija already had two pocketfuls of souvenirs, all purchased for the princely sum of a dollar.

She had left Antigua late that morning on a special tourist bus. It had cost ten times the ludicrously cheap fare on the local buses, but a visit to the Mayan site of Iximche had been included in the price, and for that reason she had not resented paying the extra. The site had been interesting enough, but watching the crowded local buses on the road she had come to regret not taking one. It would have been more like travelling in Guatemala, less like travelling through it. And the wonderful views, culminating in that first breathtaking panorama of the lake as the road wound down from Sololá, would not have been any less spectacular.

The bus had arrived in Panajachel soon after noon, and after getting a room at the hotel Chris had recommended she set out to explore the 'village', most of which was now given over to the various functions of tourism. A lovely old church survived at the end furthest from the lake, but the kilometre-long road which ran down to the shore was lined with tour companies, restaurants and stall upon stall selling the brilliantly coloured Mayan Indian artefacts in dizzying profusion. There was too much, really, and it was all a little too touristy. Or it seemed that way until she saw the lake.

Hajrija had no trouble believing that Atitlán was the most beautiful lake in the world. The deep blue-green waters were a perfect complement to the pure blue sky, and the clouds which perched like haloes above the volcanoes seemed to have been placed there by either God or an exceptional artist. She had stood gazing at it all for a long time, simply drinking it in, and wishing Razor was there to share it with her.

She was marvelling still, as the light faded from the sky. At the other tables everyone was speaking in hushed murmurs, as if they were in church. Only the little Indian girls seemed immune, and they presumably witnessed this scene every day of their lives.

As the first pinpricks of light glimmered in the darkening firmament Hajrija ordered another Cuba Libre, and thanked whatever lucky stars had brought her to Guatemala.

The transferred call from Uspantan reached Colonel Serrano's home in the middle of the family dinner. He excused himself with some relief – one more argument between his wife and daughter about the latter's lifestyle and he would seriously consider eating in the Palacio Nacional canteen.

In his study he listened patiently to Osorio's angry account of the altercation with the Englishmen, then gave him a verbal rap on the knuckles. 'Colonel Cabrera acted correctly,' he told the younger man coldly. 'We need the co-operation of the Englishmen, and that means we must take account of their sensitivities, no matter how misplaced they might be.'

Osorio said he understood that, but . . .

Serrano wished him goodnight and replaced the receiver, but made no immediate move to reclaim his seat at the head of the dining-room table. There was something seriously wrong with Osorio, he thought, despite the young man's impeccable breeding. Or maybe because of it. The man seemed to have no centre: one minute he was turning to Evangelism, the next to pleasures which Serrano found dangerously perverse.

But he did understand Osorio's anger at the Englishmen's behaviour. The hypocrisy of it! When the English had colonized North America, the Indians had been virtually wiped out. In Australia they had left the native inhabitants to rot in the desert. In South Africa they and the Dutch had invented apartheid.

Serrano reached for his cigarettes, remembered he was officially in the middle of dinner, and put them back. If Guatemala had killed all its Indians the way the *norteamericanos* had killed theirs, then who would the Anglos in Hollywood have to do all their cooking and cleaning?

Razor and Chris were woken in the small hours by Gómez, presented with Colonel Cabrera's compliments, and asked to be ready for departure in fifteen minutes. They cursed their way through the routines of dressing, weapons-checking and make-up, and emerged into the cold mountain air with a minute to spare. The same four trucks were waiting in line on the parade ground, exhausts spewing yellow smoke into the glow from the headlights.

Once again the two SAS men were gestured into the second truck, and within minutes the convoy was making its way down the hill and through the town.

'They have found a guerrilla unit,' Gómez explained in English.

'Where?' Razor asked, thinking as he did so that two days ago Gómez would probably have used 'we', not 'they'.

'In the mountains,' Gómez said vaguely. 'Not very far from the place we try the ambush. Maybe two hours in the truck, then an hour on foot.'

'How were they found?' Chris asked, but Gómez didn't know.

The trucks rumbled on, bouncing the twenty-odd men up and down like a team of synchronized kangaroo-impersonators.

'Why the hell don't they use choppers?' Chris wondered out loud.

'Too noisy, maybe?'

'This is quiet?'

'Weather conditions then. These mountains always seem to be draped in clouds in the early morning – must make landings difficult.'

It was almost four o'clock when the convoy reached its destination, the front yard of what looked, in the dark, like a deserted estate. The company formed themselves into a column and moved off, heading across abandoned fields. Visibility was not much more than a hundred metres, confirming Razor's hypothesis.

They marched for the hour Gómez had promised, and then for the best part of another. Most of the route lay uphill through forest, though sometimes they had to traverse bare and stony slopes. The temperature seemed to drop steadily as the altitude increased and dawn grew nearer. The mist seemed to thicken, though bare patches would still present themselves, allowing views of the long column stretching away to both front and rear. But for most of the time there was no real sense of the surrounding terrain: it was like marching through a cloud. Whoever their guide was, he probably deserved a medal.

Even on a bad day, Razor thought, the Brecon Beacons would have a hard job competing with this. He cheered himself up with the thought that the chances of their being ambushed by the guerrillas had to be pretty remote.

That optimism began to fray at the edges when the company reached its deployment point. 'There is an old fort halfway up this hill,' Colonel Cabrera explained to them, 'and we have reason to believe that a unit of *subversivos* is hiding out there now.'

'What reason?' Razor asked bluntly.

'There are several indications.' He counted them off on his fingers. 'One, we have satellite intelligence which points in this general direction. Two, there are reports of theft from a nearby village. Three, smoke was spotted early yesterday evening by a routine reconnaissance flight. Four, an informant has told us that this place is frequently used by the *subversivos*.' He shrugged. 'It looks promising, yes?'

'Uh-huh,' Razor said noncommittally. 'Can I see the map?'

Cabrera looked slightly surprised by the request, but passed both map and torch to the SAS man. The old fort had been marked with a red cross, and two lines of approach pencilled in. Other lines, drawn in a rough circle around the mountain, apparently represented a perimeter ring. Razor checked the scale. The ring had to be at least two kilometres long, which was a lot of ground for, say, half the company to cover. And the contour lines showed that the slopes of the mountain were streaked with deep ravines, any one of which could offer an escape route for encircled guerrillas.

'Are you going to wait for the mist to clear?' he asked Cabrera.

The hovering Osorio gave the two Englishmen a pitying look. 'We would lose the element of surprise,' the colonel replied.

A few minutes later the two SAS men joined the rear of the right-hand column and began the ascent of the steep mountain path. It was now almost six o'clock, and the mist, though no thinner, was perceptibly lighter. As they climbed up through it, feeling like disoriented divers searching blindly for the surface, Razor began to feel his sixth sense twitch with foreboding.

A couple of hundred metres above them Emelia Xicay stared over the lip of the trench which she and Jorge had dug the previous evening. Visibility was less than thirty metres, but she had a perfectly adequate view of the path below, which narrowed to a metre or so as it wound between the steep outcrop and precipitous drop. The Kaibiles would have no choice but to climb this section of the path in single file, in full view of the two trenches and their four *compa* rifles. Always assuming they came.

For the moment she could hear nothing but the slight breeze in the trees behind her. Even the birds had fallen silent, as if they knew what was coming. She imagined the soldiers further down the mountain, slowly climbing the path. It had been Kaibiles who had killed her mother, and the thought of falling into their hands made her shiver.

She looked round at Jorge, whose face betrayed the fear she felt, and they grinned at each other almost sheepishly. How good it would be to talk, she thought. The previous evening the four of them had played tapes on José's boom box and sang along as they dug the trenches, lit a fire and cooked a meal, talked and laughed . . . They had done all the things a *compa* unit could never usually do, and it had felt like a small piece of heaven, a small piece of ordinary life.

How much more of their lives would they have to spend in silence, in hiding?

She looked at her watch. In an hour or so the sun would begin to burn away the mist, and then they would have to abort the ambush, because there was no way they could hope to escape from the mountain in the full light of day. If the Kaibiles didn't find them then the helicopter gunships would.

The path zigzagged across the forested slopes, easy in some places, difficult in others. The mist was slowly suffused with daylight, but refused to lift from the deep ravines or the treetops. As always, Chris moved forward with one eye alert for danger, the other searching for birds in the trees. Behind him, at the rear of the column, Razor was asking himself why guerrillas would light a fire on a mountain. There were only two reasons he could think of. Either they were too drunk to care or they wanted to attract attention. And from what he remembered of the old man at Tikal the former seemed unlikely.

They passed a point which Razor remembered from the map, where the path took an abrupt turn and began following the contour across the slope. In a couple of hundred metres it would turn again, and resume climbing through a series of steep hairpin bends, eventually reaching the high valley and its ancient fort.

Abruptly, Chris stopped, and turned to face Razor. 'Listen,' he whispered.

Razor listened, but all he could hear was the soft footfalls of the Kaibiles receding into the distance.

'No birds,' Chris whispered.

Razor looked at him. 'We've scared them away.'

'They've been singing all around us since we started climbing – haven't you noticed?'

Razor hadn't, but he got the point. 'I think we've gone far enough,' he said.

The two men retraced a few of their steps. Where the path dipped into the ravine to cross the stream, they took up positions which would protect them from all but the luckiest of stray bullets, and waited. Less than a minute later the mountain above them exploded with gunfire.

It had been agreed in advance that they would allow twenty men to pass the rock at the beginning of the single-file stretch before opening fire. As luck would have it there was a long gap between the nineteenth and twentieth Kaibiles, and for several nerve-racking seconds Emelia waited for one of the other three to jump the gun. But then the twentieth man stepped into view, and the sound of all four rifles firing simultaneously was like an explosion.

Each of the four *compas* had been allocated five of the targets, and being the best shot Emelia had been given the leading group. The first man was easy, and he seemed to be tumbling backwards into the mist before she heard the shot. The second was just as straightforward: apparently paralysed by the shock of his comrade's sudden demise, he stood stock-still long enough for her to put more than the one necessary bullet through his upper torso.

Then it got difficult. Her other three targets were moving, two trying to move up, one to head back. She took out the latter first, coolly knocking him back into the abyss. She felt completely cool, unhurried, dispassionate. The voice which said 'they killed my mother' sounded calm as a litany in the back of her mind – there was no anger in it, only justice. The fourth man went down on the path, tripping the fifth, who was still struggling to his feet when she sent a bullet through his left ear.

Beside her she heard Jorge's gun jam, and the curse that followed. Three of his five were down, but two more were fighting their way past their fallen comrades. She took out the second, but the first reached the safety of the overhanging rock which marked the upper end of the single-file stretch. If he felt either brave or stupid enough there was now nothing to stop him coming up after them.

Or maybe he didn't think it would be necessary. It seemed only seconds later that a grenade arced into view, clattered against the cliff face just beneath them and exploded in almost the same instant, sending up a cloud of rock fragments.

'Time to go,' she told Jorge, who was still struggling with his jammed rifle.

He nodded.

She took one last elated look at the body-strewn path and ducked back along the lateral trench which they had dug for this moment. She wriggled through the gap between the two boulders and emerged a couple of metres above the path, pausing for a second to make sure it was still empty.

It was. She leapt down, making sure she bent at the knees as she landed – this was hardly the time for a sprained ankle. Confident that Jorge was behind, she started sprinting down the slope in front of her, heading for the shelter of the mist and the trees.

She had only gone twenty metres when gunfire exploded behind her, and she whipped round to see Jorge collapsing on the path. She ran back up the slope, and was five metres from the fallen *compa* when the Kaibil loomed up between the rocks above him. She fired once from the hip, and it was the luckiest shot of her life, taking him right between the eyes. The Kaibil's feet seemed to keep moving forward and he slithered over the drop and on to the path, coming to rest with his head in his lap like a broken doll.

Emelia turned back to Jorge, despair in her heart. Blood was pouring from a huge wound in his neck. She leaned the rifle against him and reached for a cloth to stem the wound, her ears straining for the sound of more Kaibiles. He smiled at her, and before she realized what he was doing, he had fixed one finger on the rifle's trigger and manoeuvred the end of its barrel into his mouth.

'No,' she cried, but he pulled the trigger.

There was no time to feel or think or do anything. Sensing movement on the path below, she tried in vain to prise the rifle from his grip, crossed herself, and took off down the slope for the second time. This time she reached the shelter of the trees, but as she did so the first bullet ripped through the foliage above her head. She turned, sinking to one knee, and took aim just as the Kaibil jumped down from the rocks. He landed on both feet, and was bouncing back up when the bullet tore away the side of his head. Another figure appeared behind him, but ducked back after sending another shot into the trees.

At almost the same instant she pulled the trigger on an empty chamber.

Resisting the temptation to abandon the heavy gun – getting hold of them had probably cost *compa* lives – she resumed her descent of the slope, expecting more bullets to follow. But for the moment none did.

The ravine seemed further than she remembered, and the dreadful thought that she had somehow got the direction wrong began to take root in her head. Then suddenly the ravine was almost at her feet, like a river of mist flowing down the mountainside. She plunged in, and started moving downhill as fast as the uneven ground would allow.

All the gunfire had now died away, and she wondered if the other two had also managed to reach their ravine. Even if they had, there was still the rest of the day to survive inside the inevitable ring. But the positions had been well prepared – all they had to do was reach them.

And the four of them had killed at least fifteen Kaibiles. This was a victory to sing about, she thought, just as the arms reached out and plucked the rifle from her grasp.

Her heart sank like a stone. Not only death, she thought, but all the rest as well. There were two of them, and they were even joking about it.

But not in Spanish, she realized. She looked closer, and saw that one of them had the hair like a brush which her brother had described. Beneath the paint on their faces they were gringos.

'*Vas*,' the other man was saying. '*Tu vas*. Go.'

She couldn't believe her ears, but the man was waving

her on like the traffic policemen she remembered from San Cristobal. Were they planning to shoot her in the back?

'*Vas. Rápidamente.*'

She did as she was told, looking back at the two strange soldiers, who turned away from her and started climbing out of the ravine, still clutching her empty rifle.

Razor was still thinking about the girl when one of Cabrera's NCOs came to collect them, with the news that there was a body to look at. For a moment he had thought he was meeting Hajrija for the second time – the same long, dark hair, same dark eyes, same slim figure in an olive drab uniform. This girl had been smaller, and her face, on closer inspection, rounder than his wife's, but even so it had been a shock.

And they had done the right thing in letting her go, he told himself, as the two of them followed the Kaibil up the steep path. The mist was lifting now, almost abruptly, as if its work of concealment was done. Two Kaibiles went past in the opposite direction, bearing a body of a comrade between them.

They climbed to the beginning of the single-file stretch and looked up at the rampart above. Half an hour ago, Razor guessed, the latter would have been close to invisible – the guerrillas had chosen their killing ground with skill. And killing ground it was: half a dozen bodies were still crumpled on the narrow path, and at least as many again could be seen at the foot of the precipice some twenty metres below.

The girl's gun had been empty, and she had been alone, but it was hard to believe one rifle could have done all this.

Colonel Cabrera was waiting by the body. The young guerrilla had taken what was probably a fatal shot to the neck, and had apparently decided to speed things along by taking his own life. There was a gaping hole where the back of his head had been, and brains were splattered across the rock behind him. Yet the expression on his face was almost serene.

It wasn't hard to guess why the man had killed himself. Razor imagined that being taken prisoner by the Kaibiles was about as life-enhancing as capture by bad-tempered nineteenth-century Apaches. And on this particular day, probably even less so. There was rage in the air all around him, rage that someone would be required to suffer for. He felt glad they had let the girl go.

'Do you recognize him?' Cabrera asked impatiently.

'No,' Razor said. 'The man I met in Tikal would be about forty years older than this.'

The colonel snorted in disgust. The Kaibiles weren't used to failure, Razor guessed. For the first time he understood how humiliating the mere existence of the old guerrilla leader must be for Cabrera and his men.

'How many of them were there?' he asked.

Cabrera shrugged. 'Maybe twenty – it's hard to tell. This fucking mist,' he said, looking round at the sunlit slope.

Behind him, Chris was lowering himself down from the ledge above, having just been to take a look at the guerrillas' firing position. By his reckoning there had been four of them, but it didn't seem very politic to say so.

'They still have to get off the mountain,' Razor commented.

The colonel gave him a withering look. 'They will be long gone now. Back to their holes in the earth.

The fucking mist,' he said again, as if that explained everything.

The return journey began mournfully, with half the remaining company strength detailed to carry the dead, and matters continued to deteriorate. They were less than halfway to their destination when a series of distant explosions echoed up the valley. It didn't take a genius to guess the source, and the remains of the four trucks were still smouldering when they reached the abandoned estate. The bodies of the two men left on guard were perched up against the old door of the estate office.

The Kaibiles settled down to wait for the summoned Chinooks, simmering with collective rage.

'Round two to your pensioner,' Chris murmured to Razor. 'At this rate we could be here for ever.'

'This bunch can lose battle after battle,' Razor said. 'My old man can't afford to lose one.'

7

Hajrija spent the Monday morning wandering round the streets of Panajachel, looking at all the beautiful things for sale and enjoying the sunshine. She didn't know whether it was the place, the baby growing inside her, or the long hours of sleep she was getting, but she felt almost unnaturally healthy, and capable of walking for hours without feeling at all tired.

Perhaps it had something to do with being on her own. Thinking back, she realized she hadn't had more than a few hours to herself since her early student days in pre-war Sarajevo, which were now more than five years in the past. College had given way to a life in which she was constantly on call, first as a hospital nurse, and then as a member of the Anti-Sniper Unit. In the latter role all trace of privacy had vanished – the unit had fought together, lived together, slept together, like a bunch of sexless children on a particularly grim holiday. Since arriving in England she had lived with Razor, and not knowing anyone else had initially been more dependent on his company than was probably healthy.

She didn't regret a moment of those five years, but she had to admit that it felt good to be on her own for a few days. Taking stock, working out where she was in her life, checking that the happiness she had grown accustomed to was real.

It seemed like it was. And the baby made it more so. My daughter, she told herself – she was already sure it was a girl. She hoped Razor wouldn't be disappointed, and didn't really think he would be. Despite his devotion to a predominantly male profession, he was a man who genuinely liked women. And these days it wasn't so hard for girls to play football.

Life was good, she thought. The continuing tragedy of her homeland, and her enduring sense of guilt for leaving, might still cast a shadow over everything else, but it was a shadow that had lately grown faint, as if it was unable to hold back the joy of her new life. The blue skies of Guatemala were threatening to dispel it completely.

That afternoon she took a boat across the lake to Santiago Atitlán, a large village nestling between volcanoes on the southern shore. From the rickety wooden landing-stage she walked up another street lined with woven goods for sale, and populated by predatory children with the faces of angels. By the time she reached the top of the hill, and the bedlam of the food market, she felt in need of silence and a place to sit.

It was a need easily satisfied, for passing through a gap between buildings, she found herself in a wide and virtually empty square. There was a raised fountain at its centre, and on the far side a beautiful white church, complete with bell tower, colonnaded entrance and a turquoise balcony. She sat on the fountain's steps, gazing at the church and the volcano which loomed behind it.

'Another perfect day,' she thought, just as a mobile sales force of six-year-olds erupted into the square.

* * *

It was late afternoon when the two Chinooks arrived back at the Uspantan base, and for most of the rest of that day the two SAS men kept to themselves, only venturing from the privacy of their room for a quick meal in the canteen.

Gómez also seemed keen to lower his profile. White-faced and silent for most of the morning and afternoon, he failed to even appear during the evening. At breakfast the following morning the two Englishmen looked for the lieutenant in vain, before deciding that they would walk down into the town without him. The guards on the gate were loath to let them go without either authorization or a chaperone, but a call to the colonel's office provided them with the former.

In the town their reception seemed subtly different, the faces a little more friendly, which led Razor to wonder whether news of their good deed on the mountain had already reached Uspantan. He hoped to hell it had not, because he certainly didn't fancy having to explain their quixotic gesture to Colonel Cabrera and Major Osorio.

They walked right through the town and out on to the valley road, enjoying the air and the exercise. About half a kilometre down, they found a path leading up into the hills and took it, climbing steadily up the partly wooded slopes for an hour or so, until the town and base were both spread out below, shrunken by the majesty of their surroundings. Razor was reminded again of Tolkien, and almost imagined he could detect a brooding cloud of uncertainty hanging above the military base.

But Mordor had been an ugly land, and this was far from that. He remembered something Jamie Docherty had said in Bosnia: the more beautiful a country, the more ugliness it seemed to bring out in people's souls. And he remembered his own answer: 'So how come there are so few saints in Birmingham?'

'What are you grinning about?' Chris asked.

Razor told him.

The East Anglian smiled, but only for a moment. 'Makes me wonder why it brings out the ugliness in some people's souls and not others,' he said.

On the way back through the town they stopped at the Guatel office, and after half an hour of trying the operator managed to connect Razor with Hajrija's hotel in Panajachel. She was out, so he left a message saying he would call again at six that evening.

Back at the base several of the Kaibiles were enjoying a kick-around on the parade ground, and Razor asked if he could join in. Chris looked at him as if he was mad, and disappeared in the direction of their room.

The Kaibiles were only too pleased to show the gringo how football should be played, and he had to admit that they did a pretty job of it. They certainly took no prisoners on the field, and at the end of an hour Razor felt like he'd been on a pitch with a dozen Ladino Vinny Joneses. Nursing his bruised shins in their room, he decided better them than Indian heads.

At five-thirty they set out for the town again, this time in the company of a quiet Lieutenant Gómez, who strolled round the darkening square with Chris as Razor talked on the phone. It seemed an age of waiting while the hotel receptionist went to find Hajrija, but then she was there, her voice full of everything he was missing.

'And how is my lover?' she asked.

'OK, considering.'

'Considering what?'

She sounded anxious. 'Considering I haven't seen you for a whole seven days,' he said, determined not to worry her.

'I know. I count them too.'

'But you're having a good time, right?' He could tell from her voice that she was, and discovered, almost to his own surprise, that he felt no resentment of the fact that she could do so without him.

'Yes, I am,' she admitted. 'But I wish you were having it with me.'

'So do I,' he said from the heart.

'Is it really bad?' she asked.

'I guess not. We're eating OK, sleeping OK. The place is beautiful. And we haven't been in any danger,' he added, with only slight exaggeration.

'How much longer – do you know?'

'Nope.'

'I have to change my hotel,' she told him, 'after tonight this one is full of tour parties. But I have a reservation in another.'

He wrote down the number she gave him, little realizing how important it would be.

They talked for another five minutes, and reluctantly said their goodbyes. Razor walked back across the square to join the others, just as a Chinook skimmed noisily above the town *en route* to the base. He remembered Chris wondering whether the plane above the square in Guatemala City had been a simple reminder of who held the real power, and the absurd thought crossed his mind that this helicopter had been sent to cast a shadow across his happiness with Hajrija.

* * *

As the sun sank beneath the rim of mountains to the west Tomás and the Old Man finished saying their goodbyes and started off down the trail. They had about twenty kilometres to walk before morning.

Tomás was sad to be leaving the *compa* camp. The victory over the Kaibiles had engendered a euphoric mood among the guerrillas, all of whom had seen enough in the way of hard times to really appreciate a few days of celebration. The sight of smiles on one another's faces for a few days would go a long way towards sustaining them all though the difficult months to come.

The comrades were still talking about Emelia's marksmanship and her incredible encounter with the strange gringos. Everyone had a different theory as to who they were and why they were with the Kaibiles, ranging from Jorge's belief that they were mentally retarded Americans to Alicia's that they were human rights monitors sent by the UN to observe the Army's behaviour. But there was nothing on the radio to substantiate the latter theory, and Emelia herself pooh-poohed the former. They hadn't spoken like Americans, she said, and they hadn't seemed stupid.

There was a down side to the euphoria, of course – an almost dangerous leap in confidence. Tomás privately considered the UN theory a typical example of wishful thinking, and he wasn't at all sure that the Old Man's decision to visit his sister's family's village – 'while the bastards are still running around like headless chickens' – was a wise one. At the very least, he had argued, the Old Man should take someone with him.

The Old Man had agreed, and chosen Tomás. Which, Emelia had said with a laugh, served him right.

Heading down the hill, the Old Man in front of him

setting a pace which belied his seventy-odd years, Tomás found himself wondering again about his sister's reaction to killing half a dozen men. Or more to the point, her lack of reaction. It was strange, the way he felt about this: he didn't want her to suffer for doing her duty, but neither did he want her to walk away completely unscathed. A death should never be taken lightly, not even the death of a Kaibil.

It was around ten in the evening, at the close of a long and boring Wednesday, when Gómez came to inform Razor and Chris that Colonel Cabrera wanted to see them in his office.

'Any idea what about?' Razor asked.

'None,' Gómez said. He had been monosyllabic all day, as if the lengthening separation from Guatemala City and his family was weakening his ability to string sentences together.

The three men walked across the floodlit parade ground in silence. A mixture of murmured conversation, angry shouts and raucous laughter floated across from the Kaibil barracks. In the space between the lights a thin crescent moon could be seen rising up behind the whale-like humps of the mountains.

Cabrera was standing behind his desk, leaning forward over the map which was spread across it. 'We may have found him,' he said, looking up at the Englishmen. He pointed at the map. 'Tziaca – a small village about twenty kilometres north-east of here, on the other side of the Cuchumatanes. We have word that two guerrillas arrived there this morning, one of them an old man.'

'Is this source reliable?' Razor asked. He hardly needed to add that the last two had not been.

'We think so. He has a lot to lose if he's lying to us.'

'So did that man the other day, but it didn't stop him.'

Cabrera nodded. 'Some of these men are fanatics. But . . . what can I say? There is never one hundred per cent certainty in these matters.'

'What makes you think the two men are still there now?' Chris asked.

'They may not be. But the older man's sister is ill, maybe dying, so there is a good chance they have taken a risk and stayed. And perhaps they are feeling a little full of themselves too, after their good fortune on the mountain. Anyway, we can lose nothing by taking a look.'

'OK,' Razor agreed.

'Good. This time, I do not intend to use the roads. Instead, a small group of eight men – including myself and both of you – will be inserted by helicopter around ten kilometres south of Tziaca. We will then move across country and establish an observation point outside the village before it wakes. If the two men are there we shall simply arrest them. If there are more *subversivos*, then I shall call in the rest of the company, which will be on stand-by here in the Chinooks.' He looked at the two SAS men in turn. 'How does that sound?'

Razor examined the map, wondering why Cabrera was being so accommodating. Fear of a third failure, perhaps. 'What's the terrain like around this village?' he asked.

'It's a small valley. The flat ground and the lower slopes have been cleared, but the upper slopes are forested. The only track runs north, down into this valley' – he pointed it out with his pen – 'but the obvious escape route is south.

There is a path that leads up into these mountains, which are heavily forested and full of hidden valleys which these people know like the back of their hand. That's why I can't risk an airborne assault,' he added. 'Give them a few minutes' warning and everyone in the village will disappear into thin air.'

'Do you have anyone who knows the village well?'

'Someone who used to live there.'

'Then it sounds like a good plan,' Razor said. Maybe the Kaibiles would make it third time lucky, he thought without enthusiasm. Still, at least that would get Chris and himself out of this damn country. 'When do we leave?' he asked.

Cabrera looked at his watch. 'In twenty-seven minutes.'

The SAS men went to make their preparations.

'Another fiasco, do you reckon?' Chris asked, as they sat side by side on the lower bunk checking the Uzis and Brownings.

A wide grin split Razor's darkened face. 'Fuck knows. I quite enjoyed the last two.' He sighed. 'But I can't say as I fancy spending the next ten years going on op after op with this bunch of incompetent psychos. Sooner or later someone will put a bullet in me.'

'Those bastards in London can't expect us to stay here for ever, can they?'

Razor shrugged. 'They've probably forgotten they sent us by now.'

'The CO won't have.'

'Yeah, let's send him a postcard next time we pass a souvenir shop.'

Chris turned to look at him. 'This is really getting to you, isn't it?'

'Isn't it getting to you?'

'I suppose so. I guess I've been assuming that since we don't have any real options, there's not much point in worrying about things.' He sighed. 'But yeah, I guess just about anywhere else would be an improvement.'

The helicopter was a Bell 212, otherwise known as the UH1N variant of the Huey Iroquois. Razor was pleased to see it wasn't one of the more common UH1Hs, which lacked an all-weather capability. A night flight through Guatemala's misty mountains was going to be pretty hairy as it was.

The two-man crew seemed cheerful enough, if not overly so. In Razor's experience most British military pilots were certifiable, and if these two Guatemalans were anything to go by then the condition was generic rather than national.

He and Chris joined a Kaibil NCO, four privates and an Indian civilian in the passenger space. The Kaibil soldiers all grinned at them, though not perhaps with quite the same enthusiasm as on their first meeting. They reminded Chris of his mother's dog after a scolding – eager to please, but still not quite certain what it had done wrong.

The Indian did not grin at them, but simply nodded his acknowledgement of their presence. He was wearing a straw hat, woven shirt, loose trousers and battered leather sandals. He seemed outwardly calm, but Razor thought he detected anger simmering beneath the surface. Or maybe not. Maybe he just expected Indians in this country to be angry.

Outside on the landing-pad Colonel Cabrera was giving an earnest Major Osorio his final instructions. The Chinooks he had mentioned had not yet arrived, but were no doubt on their way.

The colonel climbed aboard the Huey, the rotor drone

hit a higher note, and the helicopter lifted off into the night sky. For the next few minutes they flew up through thick mist, and then the view dramatically cleared, and for the rest of the flight they were treated to the dark shapes of mountains and a starry sky. The landing was one of the softest the two Englishmen had experienced, and the group of eight jumped down into a mountain meadow.

Cutting off the helicopter's engine only emphasized how loud it had been, and it was hard to believe that anyone in this part of the mountains had not been alerted to their presence. But the distance such sounds carried had been well researched by the Americans, first in Vietnam and then elsewhere, and these days all any competent commander needed to do was factor in terrain type, altitude, humidity and all the other variables, then read off the exact distance at which any particular model of plane or helicopter would be audible. If Cabrera hadn't done as much, then this probably would turn into another fiasco.

And this time, Razor thought, they would also be outnumbered, at least for the half hour required for the Chinooks to put in an appearance. And on this side of the mountains there seemed to be no mist to hide in either.

Who dares wins, he thought. Who dares needs his fucking head examined.

They set off, the Indian in the lead, along a fairly well worn track. The crescent moon, high in the sky by this time, offered enough light to make the walking infinitely easier than it had been on the two previous operations. Much of the ground had been cleared of trees, and every once in a while they saw evidence of former occupation. At one rest-stop, beside a stream noisy enough to cover the sound of conversation, Chris asked the Indian who lived on this land.

'No one,' he said laconically.

'And before?'

He looked around, as if uncertain whether he should be speaking to these gringos. 'There was a *finca* here,' he said, 'a coffee plantation. The owner was killed . . .' He shrugged.

'Who by?' Chris asked.

'The guerrillas, of course,' the Indian said, his face a mask.

They walked on, reaching the vicinity of the village soon after two-thirty. The Indian led them round in a wide arc to a position high on the hillside, from which a watch could be kept over the whole valley. A binocular scan of the village, whose nearest dwellings were some three hundred metres away, revealed no movement. The village was either sleeping or empty.

The first proof of the former came around three-thirty, when a baby started to cry. This noise was followed by others: something being dropped, a muffled shout, the scrape of something on the ground. Then a light briefly flared, and another. Through an open doorway Razor could see what looked like hanging torches, while silhouetted figures moved to and fro. Then a fire was lit, and another, and soon several thin columns of smoke were smudging the night sky.

Two young women emerged from the house Razor was watching, and while one began washing something in a container – corn, it looked like – the other began scrubbing a grindstone. Soon both were at work grinding the corn, while a scrawny dog watched them, his tail wagging furiously.

A man now emerged, and began working more noisily on another grindstone, sharpening first a hoe, then a machete, and finally an axe. He was not alone. As Razor shifted the binoculars he caught sight of at least four other males engaged in the same activity, and shutting his eyes for a moment, he could imagine the various sounds that were emanating from the village coalescing into a strange symphony.

Soon the women were rolling the ground corn into balls for the tortillas, pans were heating on the fires, and the smell of cooking was wafting up from the village.

There was something so elemental about the scene. The sounds and sights and smells of a community waking up. The process was utterly banal, probably varied hardly a whit from day to day, and yet Razor felt almost humbled by it. It all seemed so real, whatever the hell that meant.

The sky above the watchers was showing the first hint of dawn. The families sat round in circles eating the tortillas, and drinking a steaming liquid from either clay jars or plastic cups. The dogs had already been fed what looked like scraps, but waited in hope regardless.

Then, as if propelled by inner clocks, everyone but the eldest women and those with babies, gathered their farming implements and set out through the village, calling to their neighbours as they passed. Soon there were more than a hundred men, women and children making their way through the dawn twilight in the direction of the fields.

So far there had been no sign of any strangers, let alone men wearing the olive-green uniforms of the guerrillas, and as the light gradually brightened Razor began to entertain a growing hope that their quarry had already escaped.

The few women who stayed behind were busying themselves with a variety of tasks, attending to their babies, rolling more tortilla balls, sweeping out the houses. Most of the latter were low, two-storey affairs, with the ground floor reserved for living and the upper floor for storing corn. The walls were constructed from cane, the roofs from large palm leaves, and everything seemed tied together by plant fibres.

These people don't need any lessons in recycling, Razor thought wryly, just as something moving on the edge of his field of vision caused him to shift his view through the binoculars.

Two men and a young woman had emerged from one of the larger dwellings at the far end of the village. One of the men was young – in his twenties, Razor guessed – with a compact body and a face which looked friendly even though it held a frown. He was the guerrilla with whom Razor had shared a long-distance sighting the previous week.

The other man was much older. Razor had last seen him fifteen years before, walking away across the dew-soaked grass in Tikal's Plaza of the Lost World.

Both men were wearing olive-green uniforms, but neither seemed to be armed. They sat down side by side on a well-worn log while the woman poured them something from the tin kettle on the fire.

'Is it him?' Cabrera's voice hissed in his ear.

'I can't tell from this distance,' Razor lied. He found it hard to believe he was going to give this old man up to the tender mercies of the Kaibiles.

Cabrera looked disappointed, but gestured the two Englishmen to follow him down into the gully which lay just behind their observation point. 'Where do you think we should go from here?' he asked.

He was still covering himself against the possibility of another fiasco, Razor thought.

'Flush them out,' Chris suggested. 'From what I can see there's only the one obvious path leading up into the mountains – if you send a few of your lads up the track from the valley then these two will make a run for it up that path. We can be waiting for them.'

'And that'll reduce the risk of any civilian casualties,' Razor added.

Cabrera looked unimpressed for a moment, but then his face brightened. 'Flush them out,' he repeated, 'I like it. Flushing is what you do with shit, yes?'

The colonel grinned at them, and Razor knew in that instant that he could not finger the old guerrilla and live with himself. Sooner or later the Guatemalans would give him a suitable corpse to identify, and then he would be able to say yes, but there was no way he was giving up a living prisoner to the Kaibiles.

'Three men on the track, and the other five of us waiting on the path,' Cabrera was saying, apparently to himself. 'The three on the track can take some hostages in the fields, just in case these two decide to fight it out in the village.'

He went to give the orders, leaving Razor and Chris looking at each other. 'Ve vas only obeying orders,' Chris said with a mock-German accent.

'Maybe we can limit the damage,' Razor said quietly. 'Cabrera must have some notion of PR.'

'Yeah, he thinks it stands for pillage and rape.'

Razor smiled in spite of himself.

Cabrera returned with two of the Kaibiles and the Indian, who once more led the way. They had only about five hundred metres to travel as the crow flew, but the actual journey, which involved crossing a high ridge and then circling back down across a wide forested slope, was about four times as long. Cabrera constantly urged greater speed, for fear that the two men would escape while they were *en route*.

They reached the path at a point about half a kilometre above the village, and started looking for an ambush-friendly location. The trees, most of which seemed to be either pines or beeches, were far from densely packed, so they cautiously followed the direction of the village, looking for a sudden change in elevation which would offer concealment. They found it at the top of a small waterfall, where rough steps had been cut and kept by generations of village-dwellers. A man coming up them would see nothing of what was waiting at the top until it was too late.

The five men took advantage of what cover the vegetation offered and settled down to wait. Razor could not see the village from his position, but he could see the rest of the valley stretching into a distant green haze. His mind replayed the scenes of the village waking up: the child fondling the dog's ear, a woman squatting beside a fire with a flat pan full of tortillas, the man running his finger down the sharpened axe blade. And he thought about the SAS, and the rigours of the selection process they were all so proud of, and how they had been trained to endure conditions that would kill mere mortals.

Such conceit. In these mountains life was an endurance course from the cradle to the grave, and the penalty for failure was death.

He wished he was in the East Stand at White Hart Lane, twelve years old again, praying at the shrine of the great god Chivers for something as straightforward as a last-minute winner.

The sun appeared above the ridge away to their left. Half

an hour went by, then another fifteen minutes, and Razor could almost feel Cabrera's frustration reaching out across the ten metres that separated them. But there had been no word on the walkie-talkie from the other group, so there was no reason to think anything had gone wrong.

Maybe it had taken the three Kaibiles longer than expected to reach the track, Razor thought. Maybe they had stopped for a picnic, or defected to the guerrillas . . .

The sound of panting emerged from the auditory background of the waterfall, growing louder with each few seconds. A head came into view, an old man's head, with a deeply lined face and eyes that time and the wind had almost closed. He reached the top step and looked around, but either his eyesight was bad or the ambush was better concealed than Razor thought, because he showed no alarm. He was apparently unarmed.

The younger man was. His rifle appeared before he did, clambering over the rim and taking a deep breath.

'Drop the rifle,' Cabrera said. 'You are surrounded.'

As if on cue the two Kaibil privates stepped out on either side of the two guerrillas, their sub-machine-guns raised.

Slowly, reluctantly, the two men raised their hands above their heads. The young one was looking angrily at the Indian guide, but there was no anger in the Old Man's expression, just a resigned twist of amusement.

One of the Kaibiles yanked the pistol from the younger man's belt, picked up the rifle, and retreated a few steps.

Razor became aware of Cabrera's expectant look, and took a mental deep breath. He had to sound convincing . . .

'We meet again, Englishman,' the Old Man said conversationally, pulling the rug out from under his own feet.

'So it seems,' Razor said, his heart sinking.

'It is *him*,' Cabrera exclaimed triumphantly. He looked at Razor, and the look said: 'You knew, and you weren't going to tell me.' He walked forward until he was only a metre or so from the Old Man, looked him over from head to toe, and burst out laughing. 'Keeping you alive is going to be the real challenge,' he said.

He walked away, still shaking his head with amusement, and stood for several moments looking down at the village from the top of the waterfall. Then he spun abruptly round. 'Call in the company,' he told the Kaibil with the radio equipment.

'What for?' Razor growled. 'Those people haven't done anything.'

Cabrera stared at him for what seemed a long time before deigning to reply. 'They have harboured terrorists,' he said coldly, 'but that is no concern of yours. You have done your job – and now you can go home. Galvez,' he said, addressing the other Kaibil, 'you will escort our guests back to the helicopter.'

Razor stood his ground. 'For every village you destroy there will be another fifty guerrillas in the mountains.'

'And how do you work that out?' Cabrera asked, as if he was humouring a child.

'That's what has happened in every war like this for the last fifty years.' He glared at the Kaibil colonel. 'And the British Government was assured that this operation would be conducted with due . . .'

'Fuck the British Government,' Cabrera said contemptuously. 'That operation is over,' he added. '*Finito*.'

'You're nothing but a fucking butcher,' Razor told him.

Cabrera's face reddened with rage. 'No one kills seventeen of my men and gets away with it,' he hissed. 'If I had my way

I'd kill every Indian man, woman and child in this fucking province. And then I'd move on to the next one.' He turned on the hapless private. 'Send the message,' he ordered.

Razor looked at the ground, mental pictures of the villages above Zavik crowding his mind. The pile of charred remains inside the ruined church, the villagers crucified on the wall of the barn. Hajrija's Bosnia, someone else's Guatemala. He could either walk away or . . . or what? There was only one way to stop Cabrera – anything less drastic would probably end with Chris and him being thrown out of the Huey on the way home. It was all or nothing.

But where, he wondered, could they run to?

Sometimes you just had to make it up as you went along.

The Kaibil had the radio set up for transmission – there didn't seem to be time for mapping out possible consequences. Razor took a deep breath, and looked across at Chris. Finding what he hoped was acquiescence in his partner's eyes, he took a great leap into the unknown, bringing up the stubby barrel of the Uzi and pulling the trigger in one smooth motion.

Colonel Cabrera's mouth was still opening when the first bullet crashed through his front teeth and out through the back of his head, toppling him, straight as a plank, back over the lip of the waterfall. There were several thuds as his body bounced down the fall, ending with a large splash as it landed in the small pool below.

The two Kaibil soldiers were still staring after him, their faces drawn in identical lines of astonishment, as if their colonel had been suddenly summoned to the underworld by some supernatural force.

The two guerrillas looked no less surprised, though

something like a smile was breaking out on the Old Man's weathered face.

Chris shook his head. 'Another fine mess you've got me into,' he muttered.

Razor looked at him, a sudden sinking feeling in his stomach. Hajrija, he thought. How was he going to reach her?

8

The waterfall sounded louder in the silence.

'This is the third time in five years I've suddenly found myself *persona non grata* in someone else's country,' Chris observed.

'You must be doing something right then,' Razor said absent-mindedly. His mind was racing through the problems created by Cabrera's sudden demise, looking for solutions, establishing priorities. One, how were they going to deal with the three Kaibiles in the village below? Two, how were they going to get out of the immediate area? Three, how were they going to get out of the goddamn country? Four, how was Hajrija going to get out of the goddamn country?

If they were going to find answers for three and four they would need help from the guerrillas.

For their part, Tomás and the Old Man were still recovering from the double shock. One moment they had been happily on their way home to a triumphant unit, the next confronting certain torture and death. And then, before this terrible sentence had even begun to sink in, they had been granted a sudden reprieve by the mystery gringos.

It was the Old Man who recovered first. 'How many Kaibiles are there in the village?' he asked.

'Three,' Razor told him. 'And there's another eighty waiting on the helipad at Uspantan.'

'The three down there will have heard the shot,' Chris added.

'Are they in contact with Uspantan?' Tomás asked.

It sounded to Razor as if they were discussing a game. 'No,' he said. He walked across to the Kaibil with the walkie-talkie, who was standing almost rigid with fear, and relieved him of his recoilless rifle. 'I want you to talk to your sergeant,' he told the man. 'Tell him you have captured the guerrillas – sorry, *subversivos* – but that Colonel Cabrera has been wounded. Get them up here, pronto.'

The Kaibil took a deep breath and nodded.

'No heroics,' Razor told him.

The man did well, considering. Razor herded him across to join the other Kaibil, who had been disarmed by Chris, and told both men to lie face down in the grass.

'What about chummy here?' Chris asked, indicating the Indian guide, who was sitting with his head in his hands.

The Old Man spoke to him in a language the Englishman could not understand, eliciting a long reply which seemed half defiant, half resigned. 'They have his sister in the city,' the Old Man eventually translated. 'He says his sister will die now, which makes him sad, but he is glad you shot the Kaibil colonel.'

Christ almighty, Razor thought.

'Speaking of the devil, we'd better get his body back up here,' Chris said.

'Yeah, but what do we do with this guy?' Razor asked, looking at the guide.

'We will take him with us,' the Old Man said.

'OK.'

'I will help you,' Tomás told Chris. The two men disappeared down the steps, leaving Razor and the Old Man to watch the prisoners.

'The eighty men at Uspantan, they will come eventually,' the Old Man said. 'We have to warn the village.'

'Yeah.' Razor breathed out noisily, possibilities jostling each other in his mind.

Chris and Tomás reappeared, hauling Cabrera's corpse by the ankles, and dragged it another twenty metres further up the path. They then transferred the two Kaibil prisoners and the guide to the same location.

'I'll look after them,' the Old Man volunteered.

The other three took up their ambush positions, each grateful for the chance to get their thoughts back in some sort of order.

Razor was already struggling to suppress an insidious sense of panic. He was pretty certain that he and Chris could simply walk their way out of the country. They couldn't be much more than a hundred kilometres from the border, and the terrain in between was wild enough to hide an army. The two of them knew how to live off the land. Three nights and they would be in Mexico. But Hajrija was in a town fifty kilometres to the south. There was no way he or Chris could travel on the roads or survive in the towns without help. Both of them were too tall, and Chris was too fair-haired. And every policeman and soldier in Guatemala would be looking for them.

Razor hoped the guerrillas were feeling grateful.

Ten metres away Chris was wondering why he felt so calm. Because his subconscious had been expecting it, was the answer that came to mind. They had been on a collision course with their Guatemalan hosts since day one, and here was the collision. In some strange way he felt they had vindicated themselves. No doubt the men in London would see things differently, but this was the way his SAS was supposed to operate. They might not always fight on the side of the angels, but they weren't supposed to serve as auxiliaries to the scum of the earth.

And they could get out of this, no problem. Three or four days' bird-watching in the mountains – he might get to see a quetzal after all – and then . . .

Chris suddenly came to the realization that Razor had reached several minutes earlier. 'Christ,' he murmured softly to himself, just as the sound of voices drifted up from the path below. 'How much further?' one of the Kaibiles was loudly complaining in Spanish.

They clambered unwittingly over the top step, just as the two *compas* had done, and were still getting their breath back when Razor's voice told them to lay down their guns.

One man started to do so, another stood stock-still, the third's finger clenched on a trigger, sending a spray of bullets into the trees.

A bullet from Tomás's rifle knocked him backwards into the other two, his SMG firing a death-rattle at the sky. The two survivors, one with eyes tightly closed, tried not to move a muscle.

Razor and Tomás stood guard while Chris collected their guns, and the survivors were then escorted, dragging the corpse behind them, up to where Cabrera and the prisoners were laid out in the grass.

'I will go down to the village and tell them what has happened,' Tomás announced, and was half out of sight before the others had finished nodding their agreement.

Razor removed his floppy jungle hat and ran a hand through his hair. 'We need your help,' he told the Old Man, who raised an eyebrow in wry disbelief. Razor explained about Hajrija, who she was and where she was. 'The Army knows she's here, and the moment they find out what happened to Cabrera they'll go looking for her. I have to warn her, at least give her a chance to get somewhere public, so that people will know if she gets taken . . .'

The Old Man thought about it. 'It will depend on how long the Kaibiles in Uspantan wait before coming to see what has happened. Was there no discussion of contingencies?'

'I'm sure there was, but not while we were around.'

'Well, the nearest telephone is nearly twenty kilometres away,' the Old Man said. 'In Pasmolón, at the bottom of the valley. It is a three-hour journey . . . I don't think you would get there in time, and maybe not at all – it is an open road.'

'How about their radio?' Chris suggested.

'Ah, of course.' The Old Man's eyes lit up. 'Tomás is our expert in these things,' he said, 'but I see no reason why he cannot call our people. Then they can get a message through to Panajachel.'

'Great,' Razor said, wondering how long it would be before Tomás came back. 'Don't you know the frequencies?' he asked the Old Man, who shook his head.

'My memory is not so good,' he said. 'But Tomás will not be long. Do you know what message you wish to send?' he asked.

'Christ, no.' Razor ran a hand through his hair again. Think, he told himself, think.

'Could your people get her from Panajachel to our embassy in Guatemala City?' Chris interjected.

The Old Man considered the question. 'Maybe, but I wouldn't advise it. If they want her that badly they'll just go in after her, and, forgive me for saying so, but your Government will not be very popular when this news comes out. It won't be hard to fake some sort of protest mob.'

And she was still a Bosnian national, Razor thought. If the embassy wanted to hand her over they had the perfect excuse.

'I think it would be best just to move your wife to a safe place,' the Old Man said. 'And to move ourselves to one too,' he added. 'Once we have done that we can decide on what the next step should be.'

Razor could think of nothing better. There was no way he could spirit Hajrija away to complete safety, no matter how desperately he wanted to. 'Right,' he agreed. 'Thanks,' he added awkwardly.

'I think we should be thanking you,' the Old Man said, 'and when we have a few minutes to spare I shall be most interested to hear why you decided to help us. And why you were with the Kaibiles in the first place.'

'Yeah, well . . .'

Chris was looking at their four prisoners, two of whom had their faces turned in his direction. They looked like scared boys now, but men in fear of imminent death often did. 'What are we going to do with them?' he asked.

'They are Kaibiles,' the Old Man said, 'and no doubt all of them are guilty of the torture and rape and murder of our people.' He grimaced. 'But no, we do not shoot men in cold blood, not without a trial, and in this instance . . . I think, with your agreement, we should simply deprive them of their clothes and let them go. Without boots it will take them some five hours to reach Pasmolón, and the gunships will be here long before then.'

'There is another option,' Chris said, speaking to Razor. 'I'm not saying I'm in favour, but . . .' He shrugged. 'If we kill these four then there's no way the Army will know whether we've flipped or simply been captured by the guerrillas. In which case they might give us the benefit of the doubt and not go after Hajrija.'

'Shit,' Razor murmured, and looked at the sky. 'No,' he decided. 'I think the bastards will go looking for Hajrija anyway, and even if we knew for certain that they wouldn't . . .'

The Old Man looked from one man to the other, a rueful smile on his face. 'So it is decided,' he said.

A few moments later Tomás returned with the news that the village was in the throes of evacuation.

'Where will they all go?' Chris asked.

Tomás waved an arm. 'Into the mountains. They will return when the Army has gone, and rebuild the houses. They have done it before.'

'Tomás, we need your help with the radio,' the Old Man interjected, and explained what was needed.

'Come,' Tomás said to Razor, picking up the set. 'We must do this where the Kaibil scum cannot hear us.

The two men walked back to the top of the steps, from where they could see the village below. People seemed to be scurrying in every direction, all with their arms full.

Tomás examined the radio, and pronounced himself satisfied. 'I have seen these before,' he said. 'They are easy. And it is always good to get another radio,' he added, as if to himself. 'Now, tell me the message you wish to send.'

Razor went through it.

Tomás nodded, extended the antenna and turned the tuning button until the digital display showed the correct frequency. He then pressed the 'talk' button on the handset and said in Spanish: 'Emergency. Emergency. The jaguar has woken from its dream.'

'Tomás,' a female voice answered almost immediately. 'What has happened? Is the Old Man all right?'

'Yes, he's fine. We have had a run-in with the Kaibiles, but there is no time to tell you the whole story. The two gringos Emelia saw, you remember? They helped us . . .' He smiled at Razor, who smiled back weakly, and listened to Tomás's end of the conversation.

'I will explain that later . . . I am coming to that . . . One of them has a wife who is staying in Panajachel, at the Cacique Inn Hotel, and she is now in danger . . . I want you to get hold of the Santa Catarina unit, and ask them to collect her and keep her in a safe place . . . I was coming to that. There people are to tell her that Hoddle says it's OK . . . Hoddle . . . No, I don't know what it means. That's probably the point . . . We should be back sometime before midnight . . . OK.'

Tomás turned to Razor. 'We have done all we can.'

'Yeah,' Razor said. 'Thanks.' The village below seemed empty now, like a ghost village.

They walked back up the path to find the prisoners and corpses had been stripped of their clothes and footwear.

'On your feet,' Chris told them, and they obeyed reluctantly, two of them holding their hands over their genitals like footballers defending against a free kick. 'Now get out of here,' Chris told them. Hardly daring to believe their luck, the four men took a few tentative steps forward, then burst into a helter-skelter run down the path.

'What about the villagers?' Razor asked.

'They won't be taking the road,' Tomás said. 'And in any case, those bastards are nothing without their guns.'

'Time to go,' the Old Man said, looking at his watch.

Razor looked at his own: it was only just past nine o'clock. A lot had happened since dawn.

The Indian guide was waiting, his arms full of uniforms, his shoulders crossed with laced-together boots. The two SAS men and two *compas* carried their own weapons and those of the enemy. The five of them started up the slope, leaving Cabrera and his sergeant face up to the sky, a sumptuous meal for the vultures already circling overhead.

They had been walking for twenty minutes when Razor remembered the Huey.

It was not as serious an oversight as it might have been. The naked Kaibiles wasted time searching the empty village for clothes that might have been left behind, and their progress grew noticeably slower as the rough terrain took its toll on their bare feet. Still, it was only three and a half hours after their release that the four men reached the waiting Huey, stumbling into the clearing like escapees from a nudist camp. The two pilots, who had been happily playing cards all morning, managed to restrain themselves from laughing – Kaibiles, naked or not, were not noted for a self-deprecating sense of humour.

The raw details of what had happened were conveyed over the radio link during the flight back to Uspantan, and Major Osorio was waiting on the tarmac when the Huey touched down. The three men were ordered straight to Colonel Cabrera's office, where they were obliged to begin delivering a detailed report while still awaiting their replacement uniforms.

Osorio had no difficulty believing their story. He had never liked or trusted the Englishmen, and the incident of the interrogation had only served to confirm their unreliability. Listening to the four soldiers, he took a perverse pleasure in having been proved right. But this satisfaction faded somewhat when the need to inform G-2 of these developments thrust itself to the front of his mind. Colonel Serrano did not suffer failure gladly.

Still, it was Cabrera's failure, not his own. Admittedly he had devised that morning's operational plan with Cabrera, but no one else knew that. Unless, of course, the colonel had left anything in writing. Another ten minutes was wasted while Osorio made sure he had not. It was almost twenty to two when the two Chinooks lifted themselves ponderously into the sky above the base, and headed up across the mountains towards the village of Tziaca. During the flight Osorio rehearsed what he would say to Serrano when the time came.

The village was empty, of course. While most of the company began torching the houses, the four men who had been in Cabrera's party that morning led Osorio and a platoon of Kaibiles up the path behind the village. As they clambered cautiously up the last steps beside the waterfall, their eyes caught sight of the large birds perched on the bodies thirty metres up the path. When they walked forward the vultures flapped their wings in annoyance, and then took to the air, hovering in hope overhead.

The faces were still just about recognizable.

They carried the two bodies back down to the village, the vultures shadowing their journey. As the two bodies were loaded into one of the Chinooks Cabrera's head lolled sideways, and the ruined eyes seemed to reach out for one last look at the scene of their undoing. Osorio turned away in distaste and wondered what to do next.

Find them, he told himself.

He unfolded his map and spread it across the cockpit floor of the Huey, inviting the pilots to look at it with him. It didn't take a genius to work out which way they must have gone.

He looked at his watch. 'A little more than six hours,' he said. Those Indians could walk all right, but they had the Englishmen to consider. 'Let's say eight kilometres an hour. That's a maximum of fifty kilometres.' He drew an appropriate arc on the map. 'Start on this line and then follow concentric arcs back in this direction. Don't try and engage them. If you make contact, call in and hang with them. We'll join you in the Chinooks.'

The pilots nodded. They didn't seem very optimistic, Osorio thought.

Moments later he watched the Huey take off through the cloud of smoke which now hung above the burning village.

It was slightly after four o'clock when Colonel Serrano finally became aware of the morning's events on the path above Tziaca. His first instinct was to rage at Osorio – Cabrera being no longer available – but he knew in his heart that neither officer was really to blame. He should save his anger for the two Englishmen – them and all the other gringo bastards.

He listened as Osorio outlined the current state of play, and approved the measures the major had already taken:

the setting in motion of the manhunt, the general tightening of security throughout Quiche, Huehuetenango and Alta Verapaz.

How dare they, Serrano thought as he hung up. His blood boiled at the arrogance of these people. He reached for a Pall Mall to calm himself, and stood at the window for several minutes, taking deep drags on the cigarette as he stared vacantly out across the inner courtyard of the Palacio Nacional.

One dead colonel of the Kaibiles was not the end of the world, he decided eventually. He hadn't even liked Cabrera very much – the man had been too transparently ambitious. Probably trying to compensate for the Indian ancestry implicit in his dark complexion.

Serrano flicked a wrist, as if he was dispatching Cabrera's spirit into the next world. He needed to concentrate on two imperatives: first, limiting any potential damage, and second, turning the situation to his own advantage.

The first thing was to keep the matter quiet, at least for the time it took to net the two Englishmen. It was conceivable that they would need help from the English authorities in recapturing the renegades, but that wouldn't be a problem – the government in London would be as keen to keep this business out of the public eye as he was. And it would be enjoyable to pass on the news to them, Serrano decided, if only to hear the bastards squirm.

Of course, once the men were caught all bets would be off. Then their fate could serve as an example to all the foreigners who tried to interfere in the nation's affairs. They had shot a Guatemalan officer in the performance of his duty, shot him down like a dog. They would be tried and then executed, all according to the law, offering both proof of Guatemala's devotion to legality and an example of what happened to those who took up arms against the state.

But first they had to catch the bastards. Or persuade them to give themselves up. The wife, Serrano thought. He reached for the phone which connected him with the Department of Criminal Investigation offices a kilometre to the south.

She had committed no crime, but in the circumstances no one could object to the police pulling her in for questioning.

He was put through to Vincenzo. 'The wife of the Englishman,' he asked without preamble. 'Is she still under surveillance?'

'Not around the clock,' the DCI man said, sounding surprised. 'She is staying in Panajachel . . .'

'Pick her up,' Serrano said. 'Immediately. And bring her to the Palacio Nacional.' He hung up while Vincenzo was still speaking, and lit another cigarette from the previous one.

The Americans would be upset by all this, he thought. Upset with the English, but maybe also feeling a little responsible themselves. There were possibilities here.

The party of five had been walking for several hours, sometimes through forest but mostly across lightly wooded slopes. In these foothills the signs of human habitation were few and far between: traces of a path, an abandoned farmstead, a hamlet in a valley far below. The mountains marched to their left, climbing into a perfect blue sky.

The two Englishmen had not slept for twenty-eight hours, and were beginning to feel the pace. In another two hours it would be dark, Razor calculated, and then maybe they could take a rest. On the path behind him Chris had just seen his third sharp-shinned hawk of the day, its primary feathers splaying like human fingers as it soared.

They were halfway across a long, bare slope when the distant drone of a helicopter insinuated itself into their consciousness. A few stunted bushes offered the only cover, and these were a hundred metres away.

Everyone froze, their eyes searching unsuccessfully for the approaching craft. Their ears told them there was only one, and a small one at that.

'Recon,' Razor murmured, trying to get his tired brain to work.

The Old Man was pulling maroon Kaibil berets out of each trouser pocket. 'We'll have to bluff it,' he said, throwing them to the SAS men. 'Your uniforms look like theirs. We'll play dead. You call them in, get them within range.'

Before the Englishmen could reply, the three Indians were splayed corpse-like in the grass. Seconds later the Huey loomed up over the ridge about half a kilometre in front of them.

There was no way it could miss them.

Razor and Chris jammed the maroon berets on their heads and started waving wildly. Both men felt more than a little foolish. There was no way a stunt like this could work. The helicopter had seen them now, and was slowing as it approached. As the two men redoubled their efforts, they found they were laughing, and started to jump up and down, shouting abuse at the helicopter.

It was veering to their left now, but still getting closer, and they could see the two crewmen sitting next to each other in the cockpit. Neither of them seemed to be making the head movements that usually went with talking.

The range dropped to about two hundred metres, still fifty in excess of the Uzi's effective range. Razor imperiously gestured for the pilot to land.

It inched closer, like a predator uncertain of its prey. There was a movement in the cockpit, maybe a microphone being picked up.

Maybe 170 metres.

'Now,' Razor decided, and both men swung the Uzis into position, took aim, opened fire.

The helicopter jerked away, like a horse's head responding to a pull on the bridle, and at almost the same moment both crewmen jerked back in their seats.

The Huey hung suspended in mid-air for a long moment, then seemed to drop like a championship diver, twisting to strike the ground head first. The hillside exploded in flame.

The first rap on the door was so light that Hajrija dismissed it as the wind. The second got her up off the bed on which she had been reading the Mayan 'Bible', the *Popul Vuh*.

The girl was dressed in a mostly red traditional costume, and her wares were hung round both neck and wrists. She looked slightly older than most of her fellow-hawkers.

So now they were making house calls, Hajrija thought, and was just opening her mouth to send the unwelcome visitor on her way when the girl ducked under her arm and into the room. 'Hey,' Hajrija said, more than a little annoyed. She now saw that the girl was older than she had thought, more like sixteen than thirteen.

She was fishing a piece of paper from the waist of her skirt and holding it out for Hajrija.

Another hard luck story, Hajrija thought. In Antigua

several young men had approached her with requests for help with their education costs, offering beautifully printed references from some unknown college as proof of their genuineness.

She took the piece of paper and gave it a cursory look. The words 'FOLO ROSA' were printed in large untidy letters. 'TRUBAL YOU. HODAL SAY OKEY,' it went on.

'I Rosa,' the girl said. She pointed at the door, which was still open. '*Vamos*,' she added hopefully.

Hajrija looked at the letter again. 'FOLO' was follow. 'TRUBAL' must be trouble. Who was 'HODAL'?

What the hell was this?

Hoddle, she thought. Razor's hero. Almost the first thing he had shown her in England was his video clip of Hoddle's goal against Nottingham Forest. What a romantic.

But if this was from Razor . . .

A car door slammed, and she realized she had just heard it arrive in the hotel's small parking lot.

The girl was tugging at her sleeve. 'With me,' she said, 'with me.'

Hoddle said it was OK. She grabbed the travel pouch with her money and passport from the other bed and followed Rosa out of the door. The girl made a locking mime with her arm, causing the parrot necklaces on her wrist to jingle.

Hajrija locked the door, and the two of them advanced cautiously down the first-floor veranda towards the stairs. From the bend in the latter they could see two men walking around the edge of the brightly lit blue swimming pool, heading in their direction.

Rosa tugged on Hajrija's sleeve again, pulling her down the last flight of steps and then into the shadows beneath them. Seconds later they listened to the two men mount the stairway.

Again the tug, and Hajrija was following the girl through the dark hotel garden, past the empty car and out through the gates. They turned left down the road that led to the lake, making the most of the deepest shadow they could find, ears straining for sounds of a car behind them.

The thought crossed Hajrija's mind that this was some elaborate plot to rob her, and was quickly dismissed.

They reached the rickety jetty which she had visited the night before. A crescent moon was rising in the east, but was yet to cast its light on the lake, which stretched away like a sheet of dark glass towards the looming volcanoes. A small boat was being held against the jetty by a squatting Indian. He and Rosa started talking in one of the native languages, and even though Hajrija didn't understand a word, she knew the news wasn't good.

'No boat,' Rosa told her, accompanying the information with the familiar tug on the arm.

They left the man crouching on the jetty, and turned back up the road towards the hotel. Before Hajrija could question the wisdom of this direction Rosa had pulled her off through a hedge and started across what looked like an overgrown sports field. Away in the distance they could see the lights of vehicles descending the switchback road from Sololá.

They clambered across several fences in the dark, and emerged in the backyard of a family house. A man looked up from the back steps, and when Rosa said something to him he simply gestured them on with a wave of his cigarette.

At the end of a dark lane they reached the bottom of the Sololá road, just as an Army truck full of soldiers rumbled past them and into Panajachel. Surely, Hajrija thought, this couldn't all be on her account. What could Razor have done – mounted a coup all on his own?

Rosa held them there in the shadows until the highway was clear, then scuttled across, nimbly scaled the fence on the other side, and set out across what seemed like a row of backyards. For the next fifteen minutes they worked their way around the outskirts of the large village, the cliffs which lay behind it looming to their left, the lights and sounds of evening life stretching off towards the distant lake on their right.

Hajrija guessed that they were now close to the old part of the village, and a few minutes later she gained a glimpse of the church she had visited on her first evening there. The house they were making for turned out to be in one of the small streets nearby.

Their arrival produced a storm of conversation, in which anxiety and excitement seemed present in roughly equal quantities. There were two men, two women and an ever-changing gallery of children in the small back room, and all but one of the men was wearing traditional dress. After both mime and Spanish had been tried with a similar lack of success the man in modern clothes was dispatched in search of someone who spoke English, leaving those left behind to smile at each other.

The man who eventually arrived told her his name was Mariano. He spoke good English, and swiftly translated the news which had arrived from the north. Her husband, he explained, had gone with the *compañeros*, and the Army was looking for her to use as a hostage. Panajachel was now full of soldiers, in the hotels and on the roads and out on the lake. But she would be safe in this house, at least for one night.

At this point one of the women came across to Hajrija and carefully loosened her hair from under the woven headscarf she had bought that morning. 'Look at this,' she seemed to say to the others, before suggesting something which had everyone clapping with amusement and excitement.

The bad news reached the Foreign Ministry, via the British Embassy in Guatemala City, soon after midnight GMT. Martin Clarke was in his Westminster flat, having just persuaded his research assistant that they could finish their work on Atlantic fisheries law in bed, when the call from the duty officer came through. His irritation at being disturbed – it had taken four months to get the green light from this latest research assistant – was only made worse by the nature of the news.

He gathered together the clothes which he had so recently scattered, dressed, and walked swiftly through the wet streets to the Foreign Office. The Embassy report was waiting on his desk, short but to the point. The two SAS troopers sent to Guatemala to assist in an anti-terrorist operation had apparently gone off their heads, first killing the Guatemalan colonel in charge of the operation, and then defecting to the terrorists.

Clarke sat back in his chair, massaging his forehead with his fingers, and feeling the dull ache in his unrequited balls. The Guatemalans would be hopping mad, he thought. The Americans would be furious. He was furious. How the hell was Britain supposed to sell its army as the international community's mercenaries of choice when something like this happened?

If this news spread, every government in Latin America would be crying out for the blood of these men, and if they didn't get it then few of them would be falling over themselves to buy British for years to come. And if these two men *were* sacrificed then every liberal inside and outside the House would be dubbing the Government the friend of the torturers. Whichever way it went, the political outlook seemed bleak.

The fucking SAS, he thought. He would cheerfully have the whole damn lot disbanded. Who could afford a regiment that was a law unto itself? How many times, after all, did London embassies get taken over by terrorists?

Calm down, he told himself. There was no certainty as yet that this news would get out. The Guatemalans might be willing to trade silence for co-operation, since this was not likely to be very good publicity for them either. And as for the two SAS men – well, if they had gone berserk then that was their problem. The Government had no power to save them, even if it wished to. The rule of law was the rule of law.

Clarke reached for the phone, thinking that there was at least some compensation in the news – he would enjoy sharing it with the SAS CO who had treated him so rudely less than two weeks before.

Barney Davies shivered as he listened to Clarke's account of the previous day's events. He had left Jean in bed and come out to the living-room phone, but had neglected to collect his dressing-gown on the way. Whisky, he thought, pulling the phone cord after him, balancing the receiver between ear and shoulder, and reaching for the bottle.

'What do you mean, we're accepting their story?' was his first response.

'Because we have no reason as yet to doubt it. They

have the colonel's dead body and several eyewitnesses to Wilkinson shooting him in cold blood.'

Davies took a gulp of the malt and told himself to keep his temper under control. 'The reason I have to doubt it,' he said calmly, 'is my knowledge of these two men. Guatemalan Army witnesses are hardly likely to be reliable. And if, *if*, Wilkinson did shoot the colonel then he would have had a damn good reason.'

'What possible reason could he have had?'

'I don't know. These people are animals,' he added, and wished he hadn't.

'That would be your diplomatic reply, would it?' Clarke asked scathingly.

'No, it would not. Can you fax me all the information you have?' Davies asked.

'Of course. But I'm not sure what we can do for these two men, Lieutenant-Colonel.'

Davies bit his tongue – this was not the time to push Clarke, who sounded as angry as he was. 'What about Wilkinson's wife?' he asked. 'Do we know where she is?'

'No.'

'Is the embassy looking for her?'

'She is not an English national,' Clarke said coldly, 'so the answer is probably no. I will talk to you again in the morning.' Then he hung up.

Davies stood in the middle of his darkened living room, a naked man clutching a glass of whisky. 'Shit,' he muttered.

9

Less than two hours of daylight remained after the downing of the Huey, but it felt like six. If the helicopter crew had managed to get off a sighting report then the two Chinooks would be on their way, carrying eighty Kaibiles hungry to avenge their colonel. The five men marched on, climbing ever higher into the mountains, ears pricked for the swelling drone of rotor blades.

But at last the sun sank behind the mountains on their left, throwing the slopes the party was traversing into deepening shadow. They had apparently been granted a twelve-hour respite from discovery and probable death.

Another hour brought them to a wooded valley high on the eastern flank of the Cuchumatanes, and here they found the fourteen-strong unit which Tomás and the Old Man had left two days earlier. As they walked into the lightless camp the two SAS men were conscious of the curious looks they were getting from the guerrillas, though one *compañera* seemed much more interested in hugging the returning Tomás than noticing them. It was the young woman from the ravine, Chris realized.

He noticed that there were a lot of women in the camp. Almost as many women as men, in fact. And they were wearing the same olive-green uniforms.

'Will they have any news of my wife?' Razor asked the Old Man.

'No, the message went to our base camp, not here. This is just a transit camp we use sometimes. And this is only a quarter of our company,' he added. You will see the rest – and get some news, I hope – when we reach the base camp.'

'And when will that be?'

'It is a seven-hour march, so we shall leave at around eleven. Until then, you should get some sleep.'

The SAS men needed no second bidding. Oblivious to the stares of the guerrillas, they found a flat piece of ground to lie down on, and were soon sleeping the sleep of the just.

According to Razor's watch it was just after ten-thirty when a hand gently shook his shoulder, and the lovely face of the girl who had welcomed Tomás home smiled down at him. El Jefe wants to see you,' she said in Spanish, speaking slowly as if she wanted to be certain of getting it right.

'OK,' Razor said.

'She's nice,' Chris observed, watching her walk away. A waxing crescent moon had risen while they were asleep, and visibility had increased dramatically.

'Down, boy,' Razor replied. 'I think she belongs to someone else. And I don't think we can afford to piss anyone off for the next couple of days.'

'I just said she was nice.'

'Right,' Razor said sardonically, getting to his feet and looking round. The sky was strewn with clouds, but there were large stretches of open sky, black and sequinned with stars. 'Do you remember those ads on TV about joining the

Army and seeing the world? Well, I'm afraid it looks like they were true.'

Chris grinned at him. 'Let's go and ask El Jefe to send us home.'

It wasn't just the Old Man who wanted to see them – it was the whole unit. Not surprisingly, they all wanted to know what the two Englishmen had been doing with the Kaibiles.

Razor started the story at the beginning, conscious of all the pale faces gathered around him. Almost immediately several people began whispering, and for a moment he thought they must be hostile. But then he realized: the whisperers were translating his Spanish into another language, or even several of them.

He told the assembled guerrillas what their orders had been, and the doubts they had harboured, and how they had left the decision as to whether they would identify the Old Man until the time came. He talked about seeing Tomás through the binoculars at the site of the abortive ambush – this brought a laugh – and their encounter with Emelia in the ravine after the guerrillas' highly successful ambush.

'We watched the village for about four hours that morning,' Razor said, 'and I decided I was not going to identify you. But . . .'

'I identified myself,' the Old Man said, ruefully shaking his head.

'Yeah.'

'And why did you kill the Kaibil colonel?'

Razor shrugged. 'It was him or the village. Not a difficult choice.'

The Old Man looked at him, seemed about to say something, and just smiled instead. 'Is everyone satisfied?'

he asked the company. There seemed to be general assent. 'So we will help them on their way to the border?'

A woman said something in one of the native languages which made everyone laugh.

'Alicia says it would make more sense to keep you with us.'

'We are grateful for your help,' Razor said diplomatically, thinking that a man could do a lot worse with his life than join these people.

Ten minutes later the unit was setting off once more. They were heading south-west, crossing over from the eastern to the western side of the main Cuchumatanes range, Tomás had told the two Englishmen. On a night like this, he had added, it would be cold but beautiful.

They began by climbing in single file out of one high valley and into another. In Guatemala they always seemed to be climbing, Chris thought. The country was like an inverted egg-timer – when you got to the top they turned it upside down and you found yourself at the bottom again, facing yet another ascent.

But he wasn't complaining. He felt the way he had during the second half of the Bosnian mission, both heightened and torn. A heady mix of excitement and elation had accompanied him on every wilderness journey from boyhood on, and a loud echo of this was still leaping through his veins. But now it had a permanent accompaniment, almost a counterbalance. As long as he was in the SAS, this sense of elation would be tangled up in death.

He thought about the crew of the Huey, remembering their faces. He had shared a joke with one of them on the tarmac at Uspantan. They might not have been married, might not have had children, but at the very least they would have had parents, siblings, friends.

And their lives had been so easy to take. A burst on a trigger and they were gone. Just a few seconds to wonder what they would be missing, to grasp for the crucifix which had dangled in front of them on the Huey's windscreen.

Chris did not regret killing them; the choice had been clear – the lives of the helicopter crew or the lives of the five men they were seeking. But he did feel as if he had faced more than enough choices like that for a single lifetime. He wanted a chance to choose between life and death, not between one person's death and another's.

This was the last mission, he thought, and almost burst out laughing. After this one, the chances of the SAS sending him or Razor on another seemed pretty slim. Always assuming they survived.

A few paces behind him, Razor was worrying more about Hajrija's survival than his own. He cursed himself for putting her into such danger, even as he knew in his heart that there was nothing else he could have done, and nothing she would rather he had done.

So why worry? he asked himself. Because he loved her, that was why, and he couldn't bear the thought of her falling into the bastards' hands. Couldn't bear the thought of losing her.

He had never felt like this before, or at least not since he was a little boy. Then he had been frightened when his mum was late coming home, and his mind would run through all the terrible things that could have happened to her and how he would be left alone and have to go and live with his loony grandmother in her dark flat in Hoxton.

And he wondered how he could have served with so

many men who had wives and never have realized how much harder it was to risk your life when someone else needed you to come home.

'Let me get this straight,' the Prime Minister said wearily. It was just after eight in the morning, and the day was already sliding downhill. 'Two members of the SAS . . .'

'The two advisers we sent to Guatemala,' Martin Clarke added helpfully.

'The two advisers the Ministry of Defence sent to Guatemala,' the PM corrected him. 'You're seriously telling me that they've joined up with communist guerrillas? It doesn't make sense. I know the SAS have a reputation for going their own way, but that's ridiculous.'

'I know. But I don't think there's much doubt they shot a Guatemalan Army colonel. And once they had done they may have decided that the communists were their only hope of getting out of the country.'

'But why did they shoot him, for God's sake?' The PM sighed, and picked up the few remaining crumbs of pastry on his breakfast plate.

'The Guatemalans say they don't understand it either. But they do want our help.'

The PM seemed not to hear the last sentence. 'Have the media got hold of this yet?'

'No. The Guatemalans say there will be no need to publicize the matter if it is resolved quickly . . .'

'Meaning?'

'Meaning, if they catch our men soon then they'll keep quiet. Which is why . . .'

'They are threatening us with publicity? Surely they'll come out of it looking even worse . . .'

Clarke shook his head. 'With all the bad press they've had over the last fifteen years they're probably immune by now.'

The PM allowed himself a grim smile. 'You know, I can't even remember why we agreed to this scheme in the first place.'

'The Americans asked us. And needless to say, they're not very happy at the way things have turned out either.'

'Neither am I.' The PM rubbed an eye. 'So what do they want – the Guatemalans, I mean – what sort of help do they have in mind?'

'Ah. Their ambassador thinks the SAS must have routine procedures laid down for eventualities like this – you know, some sort of handbook which tells them what to do when they get stuck behind enemy lines. Will they head for the border or the coast or the embassy? That sort of thing. Will they try and steal a plane? Can either of them fly a plane, come to that?'

'Everything I've ever heard about the SAS suggests that they make it up as they go along.'

'Possibly, but it would be good to give the Guatemalans something. We can hardly claim not to know whether either of these men can pilot a plane, for example.'

The PM considered this. 'I suppose you're right,' he said hesitantly.

'I doubt if the SAS CO will co-operate,' Clarke said.

'He won't if you tell him it's for the Guatemalans. So don't tell him that. Say it's for the diplomats. Tell him we're working through channels and we need to have some idea of what his men are likely to do next.'

* * *

Barney Davies called the British Embassy in Guatemala City at 7 a.m. GMT, and spoke to a very tired-sounding military attaché. Ben Manley was not exactly sympathetic. He had apparently known Chris Martinson for years, and was both surprised and disappointed by what had happened. He admitted that it could be difficult working with the more gung-ho members of the Guatemalan Army, but that was part of the job – you didn't always get to work with people you liked.

Davies asked him about Hajrija Wilkinson, and was told that the embassy had no idea where she was. When asked whether they were looking for her, Manley first claimed, probably with some justice, that they lacked the human resources to search a country for one missing person, and then spoiled the effect by adding that they had no reason to believe she was in any danger.

Swallowing his anger – it would be better spent on other targets – Davies asked for some geographical details, particularly the last-known location of Sergeants Wilkinson and Martinson. Manley provided these willingly enough, and after getting off the phone the CO pulled out his trusty *Times Atlas*. For once, though, he found it wanting. The smallest-scale map of Guatemala was about eighty-five miles to the inch, which left the unmarked Tziaca about an eighth of an inch from Uspantan. His ruler told him that at the moment of decision the two men had been only about sixty kilometres from the nearest border, but the map gave him only the vaguest idea of what those sixty kilometres would look like on the ground.

He sent his adjutant in search of a better map, ordered two cups of tea and two rock cakes, and read once more through the faxes from the Foreign Office, feeling decidedly at a loss as to what he or the Regiment could do to help their fugitive comrades.

He was on the point of calling Martin Clarke when the junior minister called him. For diplomatic moves to be effective, Clarke told the SAS CO, the Foreign Office would need some idea of what Wilkinson and his partner were likely to do next.

'I have no idea,' Davies said, feeling instantly suspicious.

'None at all? Surely there are contingency plans for such circumstances?'

'I don't recall any of my men ever encountering circumstances remotely similar to these,' Davies said drily.

'Well, do you think they will try to get across the border?' Clarke asked patiently.

'That sounds a fair bet.'

'Can either of them fly a plane?'

'I . . .' Davies hesitated, wondering what possible need the Foreign Office could have for information like that. The Guatemalan authorities on the other hand . . . 'No, I'm pretty certain they can't,' he lied. If his suspicions were justified, then there was always the chance the Guatemalans might not bother to guard their airfields quite so assiduously. 'I'll have to go through our files,' he said helpfully. 'We're in the middle of computerization,' he added, being somewhat economical with the truth. 'So it may take some time.'

'As soon as you can,' Clarke said crisply, and hung up.

Davies took a bite out of a rock cake and reflected that British politics was like a garden pond. The longer you went without changing the water, the more scum you could see on the surface.

His two men had been sent to do a dirty job at the insistence of the Foreign Office, and he was damned if he was going to let Whitehall wash its collective hands of them.

Hajrija was woken soon after four in the morning, and while the rest of the household readied themselves for the day, two of the women worked on her. They were both in their twenties, Hajrija guessed, and their names were Lorena and Martina.

First they rubbed the paste on to her face and neck, her arms and feet. She didn't know what it was, and she wasn't at all sure she wanted to know. It didn't exactly smell bad, but it had a slightly acrid, earthy aroma. It reminded her of the herbal potions her late grandmother had concocted after day-long expeditions into the forests above Zavik. Still, whatever it was, it worked. Her skin not only grew several shades darker, but also took on a distinctly reddish tinge.

They moved on to the hair, which was the right colour to start with. The two women parted it, flattened it and braided it, giggling as they worked. Every now and then other members of the family would walk through the small room and make suggestions, compliment the stylists, or simply smile.

They were just about finished when the clothes arrived. There was a long, wraparound skirt, a long, sleeveless *huipil* tunic, and a shoulder cape, each of them beautifully woven and embroidered in the same style as that worn by the women of the house. Hajrija put them on, feeling somewhat humbled by the process. She had read enough to know that the Mayan women spent months, sometimes even years, weaving clothes that were made to last a lifetime, and she wondered where this costume had come from. She thought perhaps she could see disapproval in the eyes of the older women, but could think of no way of allaying it. She was sure it would be a mistake to offer money.

She wished her interpreter, Mariano, would put in another appearance, and allow her to express her gratitude more clearly, but when the time came to leave there was still no sign of him.

Outside it was still half dark and the dawn air, though clear, seemed damp. There were seven females in the party, ranging in age from Rosa to a woman Hajrija hadn't seen before, who had to be over fifty. She was carrying a live but apparently sleepy duck under one arm.

As the party started down the street the one weakness in Hajrija's disguise became only too apparent – she was about four inches taller than her companions. Trying to walk with her knees bent she felt even more conspicuous.

But for the moment there was no sign of the Army or the police, only similar groups of women, all laden with wares for sale, all heading in the same direction.

The bus station turned out to be little more than a large garage with two buses, both of which were already warming up. The drivers were on their respective roofs, tying down merchandise, and the crowd milled around below, chatting and holding on to the numerous live animals. Hajrija suddenly noticed the two soldiers standing to one side, and felt her heart in her mouth as one of them looked straight at her, tapped his comrade on the shoulder, and started in her direction.

He walked straight past. Casually she turned her head, and found the soldiers looking at the passports of an arriving gringo couple, both of whom had long, dark hair. They were German, she decided, though she wasn't sure why she thought so.

The driver was getting down from the roof now, and fighting his way through the throng to the door. The women accompanying Hajrija bustled forward, almost lifting her off her feet in the process, and in no time they were all funnelling aboard the bus and into seats near the back. She was given a window seat, and the eldest of the women sat down next to her, an increasingly wakeful duck in her lap.

The bus more than filled up, the minutes dragged by, and after spending what seemed an eternity adjusting his rear-view mirror the driver ground down on the clutch and squealed the vehicle into gear. Several seconds later the bus jerked forward. Emerging triumphantly from the dark cloud of its own exhaust, it began rumbling through the streets of the still largely comatose village.

They were soon out of the village, climbing the steep and twisting road to Sololá, and Hajrija was just daring to hope that there were no checkpoints when one came into view on the road ahead. The soldiers had set up a block on one of the bends, parking their vehicle in one of the lay-bys normally reserved for travellers who wanted to sit and enjoy the view across Lake Atitlán.

There were two cars ahead of them, and while they waited Hajrija became aware of the tension building in the bus, and of the various looks being cast in her direction. They all knew, she realized with a shock. Probably every Indian in Panajachel knew she was being smuggled out of the village on this bus.

And yet she felt more secure in that knowledge, not less so. Which said volumes about Guatemala; this was not just a divided country – it was two worlds, both of which happened to occupy the same geographical space.

The bus inched forward, and one soldier climbed aboard. While he checked the driver's papers another soldier started fighting his way down the aisle, which was already jam-packed with baggage and bodies. He stopped at the Germans, and laboriously went through each passport, comparing faces with photos as if determined to find a mismatch.

Failing in this task, he reluctantly handed back the passports and continued down the aisle. Acutely conscious of her height, Hajrija tried to crouch as low in her seat as possible, turning her eyes towards the window and the gorgeous panorama of lake and volcanoes.

There was a tug on her sleeve, and she turned to find her neighbour offering her the duck. Hajrija took it clumsily, then got a better hold, and concentrated on keeping her mouth closed – the white teeth were a giveaway – and her cheeks slightly inflated.

She could feel the soldier looming above them, and was expecting the blow to fall at any moment when the duck finally realized that there was a whole lake on the other side of the window. It quacked and struggled in her hands, failed to get free, and sent an avenging stream of warm shit into her lap. Hajrija half leapt from her seat with surprise, and heard the laughter explode around her. Even the soldier was laughing, holding his nose in mock dismay. He left the bus shaking his head, as if he could hardly believe it.

A minute more and they were on their way again. Hajrija's neighbour helped her wipe away most of the mess and took back the unrepentant duck. The tension in the bus evaporated as the two worlds drew away from each other again, and to her surprise Hajrija found herself relaxing like everyone else.

They passed the Sololá cemetery with its multicoloured gravestones, rumbled through the cobbled streets of the town and out on to the road which led up to the Pan-American Highway. The sun was bathing the fields now, and there were numerous groups of women walking along the side of the road, some with large bunches of wood balanced on their heads. At the Los Encuentros junction there was another checkpoint, and for a long half hour they waited in the queue for inspection. Through the window she could see other buses waiting with trucks, pick-ups, bicycles and a single Guatemala City cab, which seemed to be carrying two tourists. Everyone seemed to be heading for Chichicastenango.

Many of the drivers had abandoned their vehicles for the line of stalls selling food and drink, and the smell wafting over from the cooking fires reminded Hajrija that she had hardly eaten anything since noon the previous day.

Eventually their turn came, and this time there was no need for the duck to perform. A single soldier climbed briefly aboard, checked the Germans' passports, took one cursory glance at the rest of the passengers, and climbed down again.

An hour later the bus drew to a halt in the small town of Chichicastenango, and began disgorging its human and animal cargo. Hajrija's friends hurried her across the street and down an alley lined with stalls selling tourist goods. This fed into the town square, which possessed two whitewashed churches staring at each other across a huge market. Hajrija caught sight of a few stalls selling food and cooking utensils but the overwhelming impression was of tourist wares –

a multi-hued riot of clothes, fabrics, bags, patchwork quilts, wooden and jade carvings, purses, jewellery, rugs, brassware and wall hangings.

Hajrija's group reached the foot of the semicircular steps which led up to the front door of the larger of the two churches. Skirting round a group of women who were sitting on the steps tying gladioli into bunches, they walked up and in through the open entrance.

It was not much later than eight-thirty in the morning but already the church was alive with activity. Along each side wall, tables had been arranged, and down the centre of the nave a line of stone slabs had been laid. Both tables and slabs were covered with candles – hundreds, even thousands, of them – and the smoke from their burning was mixing with the thicker smoke of incense, drifting dreamlike in the rays of sunshine slanting in through the high windows.

Hajrija became aware that Rosa was tugging impatiently at her sleeve, and allowed herself to be led forward to where a young woman was sitting alone in one of the pews. Rosa pushed Hajrija in beside her, gave her a goodbye smile, and retreated back up the nave.

'You speak English?' the woman asked in a whisper. She was wearing a different costume, one in which green was the predominant colour.

'Yes,' Hajrija whispered back.

'I am Lara. We wait here for ten minutes, maybe twenty.'

'OK,' Hajrija said softly. She already felt reluctant to leave the church – there was something so safe about the womb-like semi-darkness, the curling smoke, the murmur of prayer. There was what looked like a whole family gathered round the nearest slab, and the father was lighting a row of thin pink candles, while the mother watched with hopeful eyes, a baby cradled in her arms.

The infant's head was encased from the nostrils up in a cloth cap, reminding Hajrija that the Mayan Indians traditionally covered their babies' eyes for the first year of their lives. She couldn't remember why they did it, but was struck for the first time at how much trust such an arrangement would engender in a child.

Maybe that was what made these people so unusual, she thought: they trusted each other. And maybe that was why she had come with Rosa the previous evening and why she had come to Chichicastenango that morning and why she was now sitting in a church pew with one complete stranger and probably waiting for another.

She couldn't understand a word most of them said, but she trusted them with her life.

When Chris Martinson awoke the sun was an orange flash through the trees, the light still almost full. He looked across at Razor, still gently snoring in the Gore-tex bag, and decided that at least one of them should have some idea of the lie of the land.

The base camp was spread across a thickly forested fold in a west-facing mountain slope. The tree canopy offered one line of defence against prying eyes, and the well-camouflaged dug-out 'accommodations' another. These in turn were widely spread, and not, Chris suspected, from any desire for privacy. Someone knew about heat signatures, and had done his best to hide the camp from American satellite observation.

He walked slowly up the hill, hoping to find an observation point which looked out over the forest canopy. He passed a man and a woman cleaning their rifles; they stared at him for a moment before raising their hands in silent greeting.

Twenty metres further up the slope he suddenly heard what sounded like someone laughing. He stopped in his tracks, listening intently, and a few seconds later the laugh sounded again. Chris started walking as quietly as he could manage towards it, his eyes searching the trees above.

He was so busy looking upwards that he almost walked into her. She stepped backwards, saying something he didn't understand. It was the woman from the ravine, he realized.

The bird laughed again, jerking both their heads towards it.

She looked at him, then pointed a finger in the direction of the invisible bird and said a word which sounded to Chris like '*ixsharu*'. 'We call it a laughing falcon,' he whispered in Spanish.

They advanced together this time, and soon Chris could see it through his binoculars, perched on a branch of a deciduous tree which he didn't recognize. The bird's bushy white crest seemed to glow in the gathering dusk, and the dark face mask looked almost owl-like.

Chris offered the binoculars to the woman, who let out almost a purr of pleasure when she caught sight of the bird. For several minutes they passed them to and fro, until the bird either grew tired of being watched or suddenly became aware of their presence, and with one last laugh flapped awkwardly up through the branches and out of sight.

She looked up at him, both pleasure and surprise in her expression. 'You know birds?' she asked doubtfully.

Everything she had ever learned about the gringo world suggested a distrust of nature.

'Yes, I do. I watch them wherever I go.'

'I watch wherever I go.'

They smiled at each other. 'I have a book with me,' Chris said, 'with pictures of birds that live in Costa Rica. And many of them live here in Guatemala too. Would you like to see it?'

'Pictures of birds?' she echoed, her eyes lighting up. 'Please, yes.' They started back down through the trees together. 'I am Emelia Xicay,' she said. 'My brother Tomás walk with you from Tziaca.'

'I am Chris Martinson,' he said.

They found Razor in the act of waking up. 'I dreamed I was Doctor Who,' he said, and then noticed Emelia. 'But your dream was obviously better than mine,' he told Chris, who was delving into his bag for *Birds of Costa Rica*.

Emelia took the proffered book with both hands, almost as if she was receiving a religious object. Then she squatted down and began slowly turning the pages, holding her eyes close in the declining light, a finger working its way through each gallery of birds. Chris and Razor watched her, both wondering the same thing – how could this be the woman who had piled a mountain path high with Kaibil dead in not much more than a minute?

'This is beautiful,' she said, in a voice which suggested the word itself was utterly inadequate.

Chris was only prevented from giving her the book on the spot by the appearance of her brother. 'Emelia,' he said, surprised to find her there.

'Tomás, look at this,' she said.

He did so, and made a mental note to find her something

like it the next time he was in the city. Though where the money would come from . . .

'Yes it is,' he agreed, and turned to tell the Englishmen that the Old Man wanted to see them.

They left Emelia fighting a losing battle with the light and walked diagonally down through the forest for some three hundred metres. The Old Man was sitting with his back against a tree, thoughtfully smoking a cigarette, a book in his lap. From the camouflaged dug-out nearby came the unmistakable drone of a generator.

'Sounds good, doesn't it,' he said as they approached. 'If Jorge can fix it properly, and we can find enough fuel, I shall retire up here and watch football on TV.' His face screwed up in self-amusement, and then abruptly grew serious again. 'Sit down,' he told them, indicating the neatly stacked cut logs which obviously served as seating for guerrilla conferences. 'Your wife is safe,' he told Razor without further preamble.

Razor closed his eyes and clenched a fist. 'Where?' he asked.

'She's in Chichicastenango at the moment. About forty-five kilometres south of here. But I'm afraid it looks like she'll have to stay there for several days, maybe even weeks.'

Razor waited for the explanation, saying nothing.

'The people who got her out of Panajachel are Cakchiquel, and though they go to the market in Chichicastenango they do not know the Quiche lands or speak Quiche. It is one of the curses of our struggle, that we are united in everything but language. Men like Tomás here, who speak Spanish and more than one of our native languages, are very rare.' He sighed. 'So, the people who are looking after your wife would find it difficult at the best of times to bring her north to us, and these are not the best of times.' He grinned suddenly. 'Depending on your point of view, that is. Your action in killing the Kaibil colonel has not gone unnoticed, my friends. In fact, it has been like throwing a very big stone into a lake, and the ripples are still spreading. The authorities know that your wife has gone into hiding, and they know she must try to reach a border or an embassy or us. And as part of making sure she doesn't reach us, the Army is searching every town and blocking every road between Atitlán and the Cuchumatanes. If she stays where she is I think she will be safe, but if she tries to move . . .' He shrugged. 'Better she stays.'

Razor looked doubtful. 'So what do we do – just wait?'

'No. I think you two should start for Mexico tonight. Two of our *compañeros* will go with you and . . .' He stopped, noticing the look on Razor's face. 'Once you two are in Mexico they will not need your wife for leverage,' he said.

'Just for revenge,' Razor said. 'I'm sorry, I know what you say makes sense, but I can't leave her behind. I can't. I won't. If this Chichi-place is only forty-five kilometres away then all I need is a good map. I can get there across country in two nights.'

'We can,' Chris corrected him.

'No way,' Razor said. 'You should either head for Mexico or stay here, because if both of us are taken then there'll be no one to call in the cavalry.'

'And which cavalry is that then?'

'You know what I mean. People disappear in this country, and I kind of like the idea that someone will know to look for me.'

'Yeah, OK.'

'But I will go with you,' Tomás said unexpectedly. He owed the Englishmen his life, he thought. And he owed them for Emelia's too. But most of all he felt a fascination with this strange gringo, this soldier who had decided on the spur of the moment to risk everything for a village he had never seen before, and who danced like a madman to lure a helicopter to its destruction.

He turned to the Old Man. 'If the unit can spare me,' he added, by way of asking permission.

The Old Man looked at him, and seemed to guess what was in his heart. 'We can spare you,' he said, 'but not permanently. Be careful.'

10

The sky was clear as the two men began their journey, their path down the mountain illuminated by a piercing moon. Far below them coils of mist shone like silver snakes in the dark folds of the foothills.

Razor's initial sense of relief at discovering Hajrija was safe had worn off, and anxiety was gnawing away at the edges of his mind. The authorities might not have found her in Panajachel, but if the Old Man's sources were accurate, they were not going to stop looking. At this very moment they might be battering down the door of the house in which she was hiding.

He asked himself for the hundredth time how he could have put her in such danger. He should never have let her come to Guatemala with them. Such bloody arrogance. And now here he was heading out to rescue her like a knight in fucking armour. Was this another mistake? More overconfidence? For the first time in his professional life Razor felt besieged by self-doubt.

He knew that his effectiveness in situations like this had often come from an almost ludicrous surfeit of confidence. They all laughed at the Regimental motto, but in his case it had been almost prophetic. Every time he had dared, he had won. The trouble was, in order to make the dare effective you had to be prepared to lose, and he only had to think about it for five seconds to know that he wasn't prepared to lose Hajrija.

If Cabrera had given him another five seconds to consider the consequences he might still be alive.

Still, Razor had confidence in his companion. Tomás reminded him a little of Trooper Damien Robson, who had been part of the Bosnian team. 'The Dame' had carried himself with the same air of self-containment, and performed with the same quiet efficiency, as the Guatemalan. He had also, as Razor remembered from one conversation in Bosnia, been as protective of his sisters as Tomás seemed to be of Emelia. Razor found himself hoping that his new companion would have a longer life than the Dame.

It took them an hour and a half to reach the road which wound its way through the foothills, and another hour of easier walking before they came to their first major water obstacle. Nature had provided the first few stepping-stones, humankind a few more, and even in the thickening mist they had no trouble crossing the tumbling river.

'Another hour and we will have a short rest,' Tomás told him on the far bank. Two days ago he would have expected an argument, but that was before he discovered that these gringos could walk like Indians.

The going was uphill now, and soon they found themselves emerging from the mist, the fuzzy white arc of the moon growing sharper with each climbing stride. It took almost an hour to reach the next ridge-line, and here they stopped, sitting on some convenient rocks at the top of a pass, staring down at the lakes of mist on either side.

Tomás took a small stack of tortillas from his pack and

passed half across. 'Why did you become a soldier?' he asked, hoping the answer would give him the chance to ask the question which really interested him.

Razor shrugged. 'I just drifted into it. Couldn't think of anything else to do, I suppose. And I enjoyed the life.'

Tomás took a swig of water from the canteen and wiped his lips with the back of his hand. 'Can I ask you a personal question?' he asked.

'No harm in asking, as my mum used to say.'

'To be in an Army that is for the government – does that not sometimes, well, trouble you?'

'No . . . well, it never used to. The British Government is not like the one here. And most of the time we think of our Army as defending us against foreigners of one sort or another, from outside Britain. Your Army seems more interested in fighting its own people.'

'We are not their people.'

'Yeah, I know . . .'

'I understand what you say,' Tomás went on, 'but for me it is important to know what we are fighting *for*, and – forgive me – but when you are sent here to help this government of butchers and torturers I cannot help wondering what it is *you* think you are fighting for.'

Razor could see his point. To say he was just obeying orders didn't sound like much of a reason. 'I guess I have to believe that my government has the interests of the British people at heart, and that sending us here was part of promoting those interests.'

Put like that, he thought, it sounded lamer than lame. He made a mental note not to apply for a job in Army Recruitment.

Tomás was smiling at him though. 'I think your heart

told you what you wish to fight for on the day you kill the Kaibil colonel. It is justice.'

Razor grimaced. 'That was one moment. And a personal thing.' He didn't really want to think about why. Or what the British Army really was for these days. It was something of a stretch to see it as an instrument of justice.

Tomás took the hint, and even felt a little sorry for the Englishman. Clarity of purpose was something he had always felt grateful for, even when the cost had seemed so high.

They resumed their journey, hiking down into the misty valley and up towards another moonlit crest. It was midnight when they reached it, and over half the night's projected forty kilometres were behind them. Another long slope, this time heavily forested, led them down into another valley, and to another bridge of stones across a rushing river. For some reason the mist was much thinner here, and Razor could see the shapes of buildings looming in front of them.

Ruined buildings. The façade of a small adobe church was still standing among the weeds, its walls scorched by the fire that had apparently destroyed it. Twenty metres away a jumble of concrete blocks was all that remained of another building.

'What happened here?' Razor asked, although he had already guessed the answer.

'The Army came,' Tomás said shortly. 'See here,' he added, pointing at the ground in front of the church, where a large number of flower petals had been recently strewn. 'They are marigolds – the death flower. They have been left here to honour those who were killed.'

The two men walked on, the ghostly ruins fading behind

them. Razor told Tomás about the model village the Army had shown him and Chris in the mountains near Uspantan.

'I know the place,' Tomás said.

'What happened there?' Razor asked.

Tomás told him the story in clipped sentences, as if any extravagance of language would somehow mitigate the crimes which had been committed there. 'The Army came to the area,' he began, and Razor could feel the terrible weight of those few words. Groups of soldiers had started coming to the village looking for *subversivos*, and soon people began to disappear, their mutilated bodies turning up by the side of the road. Eventually the soldiers came in force, truckloads of them, with machine-guns. All the villagers were herded into the space in front of the church, and then the men were crammed into the small village hall, from where they could hear the women being first raped and then shot. After that the only sound for a while was the weeping of the children, and then the soldiers had cut out the little ones' stomachs one by one, opening the door of the hall so the men could see what was happening. The soldiers screamed that these children were the seeds of future *subversivos*, and that this was the only way to cleanse the country of such sickness. Then they took out the stunned men and slit their throats. The bodies had all been piled into the well to rot so that no one could live in the village again.

'That is what happened there,' Tomás said.

In the silence that followed Razor felt the mist like a cloak of sadness. How could such things happen? How could men behave like that? He remembered the same questions filling his mind in the villages above Zavik, but in Bosnia it had not been difficult for him and the others to justify their participation in the war. After all, the suits in Whitehall had not sent them in to help the Serb irregulars with their ethnic cleansing.

But hadn't that just been a matter of luck? If British interests had required victory for the Serbs then there was a good chance he and the others would have ended up fighting alongside them. It occurred to Razor that until now he had never really needed to ask himself the question which Tomás had asked, but that this period of grace was over, and that when he got back to England – he gave a wry smile in the dark – he would need to devote some thought to what exactly it was that he was fighting for.

For the moment, at least, he had no doubts. He was fighting for his own life and that of his wife. The fact that once again he seemed to be on the side of the angels was just a bonus.

It was now more than twenty-four hours since Lara had brought Hajrija to the house on the town's outskirts, and she was beginning to feel the strain of confinement. The old couple who lived there could not have been more welcoming – when she arrived both had embraced her like a long-lost favourite daughter – but their English was even more sparse than Hajrija's Spanish, and verbal communication was more or less impossible. So far, Lara had not returned.

On the previous day Hajrija had helped out with the cleaning, finished the small mountain of sewing jobs which had been waiting for the couple's daughter, and gone to bed early. Since waking up that morning she had spent most of her time pacing to and fro, trying to keep her mind occupied. She had already made up several stories about a big ginger cat named Hoddle that she would one day read to her daughter, and now she was telling the unborn baby about herself and Razor, how they had met, and where they both came from. She was just describing the house in Zavik where she had grown up, when there was a light rap on the door.

It was Lara. 'I have news,' she said. 'Your husband, he come and fetch you.'

'Not alone!?'

'No, no, he will be lost. One of the *compañeros* bring him. They hope to be here Monday morning. Before the sun comes.'

'What day is it today?'

Lara laughed. 'Saturday, of course.'

Hajrija felt joy bubbling up inside her at the prospect.

'I go,' Lara said, getting up. 'The soldiers are everywhere today, like swarm of hornets.'

Once the *compañera* had left Hajrija discovered that her joy had evaporated, and that new anxieties were busy tying a thick knot in her stomach.

Both men were woken in the late afternoon by the sound of the two Chinooks. They came no nearer than half a kilometre, dark shapes against the deep-blue eastern sky, headed for the towering bulk of the Cuchumatanes.

Sated with sleep, the two men waited in their covered hide for the light to fade before continuing their journey. This time there was chilli with the tortillas, but only water to drink. Razor would have killed for a cup of tea, but lighting a fire would have been akin to signing a suicide note.

'When will we reach Chichi-whatsit?' he asked.

'Chi-chi-cas-ten-ango,' Tomás said slowly, as if he was

teaching a small child, and then grinned. 'Tomorrow night, I hope. If things go well we can get your wife out of the town before dawn on the next day.'

Razor brought a picture of Hajrija to his mind, the water from the shower running down her laughing face, the love in her eyes, and the now familiar wave of panic threatened to engulf him. Think about something else, he told himself. Anything else. 'So why did you become a soldier?' he asked Tomás.

'I decided to fight for my people,' Tomás said simply.

'I understand that. But there are lots of your people who don't choose to do that. Why did you?'

'Ah, I see what you mean. I suppose most of us in the mountains have just come to a point where we can take no more, where we have no choice but to fight if we wish to consider ourselves human.'

'Are your parents alive?'

'No. The Army killed them both. My father, he was a good man who could not understand what was happening in our village. He just could not believe that the authorities would let things go on the way they were if they knew what was happening.' Tomás smiled sadly. 'Of course they knew exactly what was happening, and one day my father did not come home.' He sighed, and idly drew a circle in the dust.

'My mother understood,' he said quietly, 'but she went looking for justice. Not because she expected to find it, but because she wanted others to see that it could not be found in the way things are. At least, that is how I think she worked it out.' He gave Razor a rueful smile, but there was no disguising the pain in his eyes. 'She was kidnapped by the Army and raped by many men, and tortured. They cut off her ears and her nose and her breasts and they left her dying on a hillside, with soldiers there to make sure no one could try to lessen her pain.'

He stopped talking, and Razor could think of no way to soften the silence. 'What happened to you after your mother died?' he asked eventually.

'My two older brothers left to join the guerrillas after that, but I was only fourteen years old, and Emelia was only nine. We went to live with my uncle – the husband of my father's sister – in a village not far from here. It is about twenty kilometres in that direction.' He gestured towards the west.

'My uncle was an important man in the *cofradías*. Do you know what they are? They are a little like priests, a little like politicians, a little like community elders. They are the men entrusted with preserving the old traditions, of keeping our way of life alive. I learnt a lot from my uncle before he was killed,' he added. 'But that's another story – I think it is dark enough for us to leave now.'

The land grew no flatter, but as the evening wore on the two men saw increasing signs of human habitation: well-worn paths, areas of cleared forest, the wink of yellow lights in a far-off village. Even the rivers seemed tamer, lacking the same eagerness to reach the distant ocean.

Around nine o'clock they breasted a small ridge and saw a village almost immediately beneath them. Several of the houses were lit and, much to Razor's surprise, the sound of voices floated up into the night, singing voices, with an accordion for company. Razor could make no sense of the words, but there was no mistaking the joy with which they were being sung.

He felt close to tears, and wondered how a few happy

voices and an out-of-tune accordion could move him so much, when the tragedies recounted by Tomás had left him with only cold rage and a sense of hopelessness. But maybe that was obvious – in a heart of darkness nothing is more moving than a light being held aloft.

'We have friends here,' Tomás said, and led the way down the slope, stopping every few metres to look and listen. They were within fifty metres of the first house when two figures suddenly appeared in front of them. Tomás said something in the local language, and the men hurried forward to embrace him.

He introduced Razor, and they shook his hand with enthusiasm, all the while staring up at him with the wonder of men greeting a well-meaning traveller from outer space. Razor smiled back, and then took a back seat as Tomás listened to what the men had to tell him. In the village the accordion had fallen silent, but the voices were still filling the night air with their bitter-sweet beauty.

A few minutes later the two villagers were heading back towards the houses. 'An army patrol went up the next valley this afternoon,' Tomás told Razor, 'but my friends don't know where it was going. Otherwise they say all the activity has been north of here.' His teeth flashed white in the darkness. 'The army told one of the villagers they're looking for a couple of crazy gringo criminals. American drug-runners.'

In his study Colonel Serrano pored over the small-scale military map, mentally measuring distances in time. If the woman had been in Panajachel, the two men north-west of Uspantan . . . But how did they get her out of Panajachel? He looked again at the surveillance photos which had been taken in Antigua. She was wearing blue jeans, a white T-shirt and a beige jacket. Dark glasses perched on top of the swept-back hair. A good suntan for someone who had only just arrived . . .

So it wasn't a suntan. Señora Wilkinson had naturally dark skin and black hair. They had disguised her as an Indian, Serrano realized, and probably taken her out on a bus.

His finger followed the road out of Panajachel, through Sololá, north to Los Encuentros and then, after a slight hesitation, north again to Chichicastenango. The mumbo-jumbo town. Crawling with holy idiots and *subversivos*. If the tourists didn't spend so much of their money there the Army would have long since razed the place to the ground.

Serrano let his finger rest on the town for a second, then exchanged it for a fist, smiling as he did so.

It was almost three in the morning and the mist in the narrow valley seemed to be growing thicker by the minute. But not evenly – it was a bit like his mum's custard, Razor thought, thicker in some places than others. Sometimes the river below the path was visible, and occasionally even the steep rocky wall which lay beyond the cascading water swam into view, but for long periods now Razor's field of vision had included no more than the blurry figure of his companion and a few metres of rocks and grass on either side of the path.

Given the noise the river was making, the two men were lucky to hear the advancing patrol. Later they were unable to agree on exactly what it was they had heard – Tomás claimed that someone had laughed, Razor that the man had cursed – but whatever it was it stopped both men in their tracks as if they had hit an invisible wall.

The noise had sounded so close, but all they could hear was the river, and all they could see was the wall of grey. Both men made the same mental calculations, and simultaneously gestured each other off the path in the direction of the water. The grass and rocks were slippery, the descent decidedly uneven, and they half scrambled, half fell the twenty metres or so, ending up crouching precariously a few feet above the swirling black water.

No more sounds had emerged out of the mist, and they were just beginning to wonder if nature had played a trick on their ears when the first in a line of dim, shadowy figures came into view on the path above. Both men froze again, inwardly praying that the view looking down was dimmer than the view looking up. The temptation to bring the Uzis into the firing position was almost irresistible, but any movement might well be fatal.

The figures filed past above them, like a long line of armed ghosts. Ten men, Razor counted. Fifteen, twenty, twenty-three. And then they were gone.

The two men waited another minute to be sure, then climbed back up to the path. Tomás wiped his brow in mock relief and turned to go, just as the figure stumbled out of the mist in front of them. The man's rifle seemed to almost leap from his hands as he tried to bring it round, and Tomás's Uzi stitched a line across his chest, throwing both man and weapon into the air.

Someone shouted on the path behind them, but the two men were already running. Razor glanced down at the dead soldier as he leapt over him, and saw that the zip on the man's trousers was undone. He had obviously dropped off the back of the line for a piss. Which had been bad luck, both for him and for them.

They ran on, listening for the sounds of pursuit, but for several minutes they could hear nothing more lethal than their own footfalls and breathing above the monotonous rush of the river below. Then a sub-machine-gun opened up in the distance, much too far behind them to do any damage.

They kept running, willing themselves on. After another half a kilometre the path wound up and out of the narrowing valley, and crossed a small high meadow where swirls of mist alternated with patches of stars, before descending once more into the realms of opacity. The two men slowed their pace to conserve energy, both knowing that when the dawn came and the mist lifted the enemy would be filling the sky with reconnaissance flights.

At the bottom of the next valley they took to the river. According to Tomás the Army never used tracker dogs, but Razor was afraid the bastards might make an exception in their case. After a couple of kilometres they left the river for one of its tributary streams, heading up a forested hillside toward its source. By the time they left the water, their feet half-numbed by the cold, first light was only an hour away, and it was time to dig in for the coming day. Tomás reckoned they were now no more than twelve kilometres from Chichicastenango.

The two men dug a rectangular scrape in a dry dip, and embellished the tarpaulin cover with artistically draped foliage. Unless someone literally dropped in to see them they would be safe until nightfall.

They slept in shifts as a precaution, but there was no need. Helicopters were audible for most of the day, but the hunt for them seemed concentrated about ten kilometres to the north: either someone had reported a false sighting or no one in authority had been able to believe they could have travelled as far as they had. Not a single patrol disturbed the serenity of their forested hillside.

At around five they shared the usual scant meal and talked about the night to come. He would take them to a hill above Chichicastenango, Tomás said, and then he would go down on his own to fetch Hajrija in the hour before dawn. Razor felt like protesting about the arrangement, but unfortunately it made sense – his height would be a give-away on the streets of the town.

'Do you know the place well?' he asked.

Tomás nodded. 'We used to go there when we lived with my uncle. His *cofradía* conducted many ceremonies in the Church of San Tomás.' He smiled. 'There are many tourists now, and perhaps it is not what it was, but that is a good thing as well as a bad thing. The less land my people have the more they need the money from the tourists.'

'But you come from near Lake Atitlán, right?'

'Santiago Atitlán. It is on the south shore of the lake.'

'So why are you fighting with the Old Man in the Cuchumatanes? Are there no guerrilla units around the lake?'

'Yes, there are: the people who organized your wife's escape from Panajachel are part of one unit. It is just chance that Emelia and I are in the north. I met the Old Man in a refugee camp in Mexico and we have been together ever since. It is many years now.'

'And how many more, do you think?'

'Until the Old Man dies . . . I do not know.'

'He looks indestructible. But can you win? Or can there

be some sort of peace? What about this agreement which the Government wants to sign with you?'

Tomás snorted. 'Their agreement is a waste of paper. The issue here is land, and their agreement doesn't even mention it. When we are strong enough to make them talk about land, then there will be a chance of peace. But I am afraid that will take a long time. Five years . . . maybe ten.' He smiled ruefully. 'It is hard to think about it sometimes. We have each other, and we know our cause is just, and our hearts are full, but all of us sometimes long for a normal life. A husband or a wife, children, enough land to grow food on, an end to living in fear. Of course one day we would like proper schools and clinics and a life that is easier, but the simple things must come first. No one should live every day of their lives in fear.'

The dusk was deepening in the forest. 'It's time to go,' Tomás said.

Hajrija sat awkwardly in the confined space, trying not to worry about the staleness of the air or the complete lack of light. She had been in hiding for two hours now, ever since a breathless Lara had arrived with news that the Army had begun a house-to-house search of the town. The old couple had taken it calmly, lifting up the rug in the corner of their main room to reveal the dug-out hole beneath.

She had gone in willingly enough, and the sound of the soldiers searching the house above her had confirmed the soundness of the arrangement, but now, three hours after their departure, she was beginning to feel more than a little disoriented by the experience. Hajrija had always thought the movies exaggerated the horrors of solitary confinement, but the sharpening edge of hysteria in her own mind suggested they had not.

And the more she thought about it, the clearer it became that the real surprise was how long it had taken her to realize the seriousness of the situation. But then again, she thought, smiling grimly to herself in the darkness, it wasn't so hard to work out why it had taken her so long. When all you met was kindness, it was hard to take evil and its consequences seriously.

Two platoon-strength units of guerrillas had left on the same night as Tomás and Razor, leaving the base camp more than half empty. For the next two days and nights Chris had helped out with the maintenance chores, taken his turn on sentry duty, and enjoyed several walks in the forest with Emelia, book and binoculars. They had neither seen nor heard another laughing falcon, but on one foray up the mountain they had surprised a Montezuma quail crouching in the grass, its boldly patterned black and white face peering out at them with almost comic alarm.

The camp's social life was concentrated in the evenings, when groups of *compas* would gather around the butane stoves on which dinner had been cooked, and then there would be talking, storytelling, and sometimes singing, deep into the night.

There would also be a great deal of flirting. Some of the *compas* were obviously partnered off, but there was no way for Chris to know how permanent the relationships were. He wondered if strict Catholic precepts in this regard had ever been adopted by the Mayans, and if so, whether the pressures of life in the mountains had led to a loosening of what was deemed acceptable.

That evening he asked Emelia.

She thought about it for a moment. 'At the beginning,' she said, 'when more than a few women came to the mountains to fight, I think it was hard for all those who had been brought up to believe sex outside marriage was wrong. And not just for the women – I think some of the men had a hard time accepting women who gave them what they said they wanted! But over the years, well, we are human beings and being in love and having sexual relations are part of being human.

'Of course, it is not the same as in a village or even the city. We cannot ever pretend we are living a carefree life – quite the opposite, in fact – and just as we must always be on our guard against the enemy, so we must be twice as careful in how we deal with each other. We cannot afford jealousies and resentments in the camp, so we must be serious in love as we are in all other things. But I think that is good.

'It is hard to see someone you love die,' she said, and the slight change of tone in her voice made Chris aware that this was something she knew from first experience.

'But of course the struggle goes on,' she added.

'Did you lose someone?' Chris asked.

'Yes, I lost someone. His name was Francisco. He was killed on an operation. A year ago now.' She stared out across the rapidly darkening vista, defiance in the set of her lips, loss in her eyes. 'It seems a long time, but it isn't.'

That explained why the men rarely flirted with her, Chris thought.

'And of course we cannot have pregnant women in the mountains,' she went on, as if determined to move the conversation away from the personal level. 'If an accident happens then the *compañera* must return to her village or the city until the baby is born, and then she must leave the child with a relative if she wishes to return to combat.'

She turned her face to his in the gloom, wondering if he could understand what she was saying.

By some unfortunate quirk the mountain bowl which held Chichicastenango was free of any concealing mist. Looking down through the pines from their position on the hill Razor could see the sleeping town spread out beneath, the two white churches standing sentry at either end of the main square.

At least the moon would soon be down, he thought, turning to look for Tomás. His companion was crouching in front of the strange stone idol which resided on the hill, and which he claimed was thousands of years old. Pascual Abaj was its name, and according to Tomás it was the local representative of the Mayan earth god, whose name Razor had already forgotten. Scattered in front of the idol were a variety of offerings left by visitors in either hope or gratitude: several bunches of flowers, a small bottle of local brandy, two packets of cigarettes and a can of Coca-Cola.

Tomás got to his feet, feeling strengthened by his communion with Pascual Abaj, and looked at his watch. 'I must go soon,' he said.

'I know,' Razor replied, looking again at the map Tomás had drawn for him. He could think of nothing more to ask. With any luck his friend would return with Hajrija before dawn, and he would have no need to use it.

The two men shook hands almost formally, and then embraced. There was an almost serene expression in the guerrilla's eyes, Razor noticed. In his own he imagined there was only anxiety. 'Good luck, mate,' he murmured, but Tomás was already disappearing down through the trees, his mind focused on what lay ahead.

They had been observing the town for four hours, and there had been little activity in that time. One three-truck convoy had passed through on its way to the north, the noise of its passage down the cobbled streets enough to wake the dead, but there had been no sign of any motorized patrols within the town itself. There might be foot patrols, but none had been visible from the top of their hill. With any luck most of the local military were still scouring the countryside, but Tomás knew he could take nothing for granted.

He reached the foot of the trees just as the moon disappeared behind the mountains to his left, casting the town into deeper shadow. Keeping low, he crept round the edge of a cornfield and through the backyard of a tumbledown shack. On the other side he reached the small road which led along the rim of a ravine and into the town. A dog barked in the yard he had just passed, as if it had only belatedly realized its responsibilities.

Tomás started up the road, one hand on the butt of the handgun that was tucked into his belt. It would have been nice to have the Uzi, but there was no way of carrying the sub-machine-gun as a concealed weapon, and there was always the chance he would need to pass himself off as just another Indian.

The road turned away from the ravine and a possible escape route. Now there were houses on either side of a steeply sloping street – a death trap if an Army patrol turned one of the corners in front of him. Tomás kept close to the buildings, listening for the sound of an approaching enemy.

At the crossroads he put an eye to the corner wall, and looked down the street which led into the main square. Almost directly ahead of him the church of his saintly namesake thrust its plain white façade towards the heavens, and he felt the weight of the memories, both his own and his people's, which the sight evoked.

He cautiously advanced to the corner of the square, and crouched down in the shelter of an empty stall only metres away from the church steps. The smell of incense still lingered in the air, and in his mind Tomás could hear the fireworks and see the Virgin Mary held aloft on a sun-filled afternoon.

The town seemed locked in silence, and for a moment he let his mind wander, north towards Emelia in the mountains, south towards the Englishman on the hill. Watching Razor try to make sense of Guatemala, Tomás had realized how narrow his own experience was. Emelia was right – it was important to learn about other worlds, and even to visit them if possible. Their way of life was not so fragile that it need fear contact with others.

After the war, he told himself. Nothing lasted for ever.

He looked at his watch – it was half-past four. He had been in the same place now for ten minutes, and heard nothing. Slipping out of his hiding place, he started out for the opposite corner of the square, turning right, then left, then right again, through the labyrinth of empty stalls.

He was two-thirds of the way across when the spotlights came on, and for a second he stood half blinded in the glare, before his survival instinct kicked in, and sent him scrambling into the shelter of a stall.

It was only then, crouching in the dark, that he realized no gun had been fired. They wanted him alive.

'If you surrender yourself, you will be well treated,' a voice shouted. Its owner could hardly keep the amusement out of his voice.

Tomás could hear soldiers all around him now, talking, shuffling their cramped legs – they had no need to be silent any more. From every side of the square he seemed to hear a hum of expectancy.

I am a dead man, he thought. There is no way out of this, none at all. I made what is mine. Including this death.

Razor would have seen the light flooding the square, known that it had all gone wrong. Tomás idly wondered what the Englishman would do next. It was no longer his concern. He had just joined the end of a line which stretched back hundreds of years, a line of deaths which brought pain to the living, that pain which life dulled to an ache and new death resharpened. He felt the pain his death would bring to his sister, but also a sense almost of relief, almost of vindication. He had stayed true, he had not faltered.

He got slowly to his feet, and stepped out once more into the light. He was sure they wouldn't shoot him – the death they had planned would take weeks, even months.

'Lay down your gun,' the same voice shouted from the shadows.

As Tomás looked up at the cross atop the church and smiled to himself, the voice in the darkness was shouting something else, but Tomás didn't hear what it was. With great care he slid the barrel of the gun into his mouth and pulled the trigger.

11

On the hill above Chichicastenango, Razor had seen the square below suddenly drenched in light, and had sought in vain for an optimistic explanation. Now, hearing the single shot echo out across the town, he feared the worst.

He fought back the urge to follow the other man down. If Tomás was still alive and free then he would return. If he was captured or dead then there was nothing Razor could do.

It was now after five o'clock, and it would begin to get light within the hour. Razor studied the road which ran alongside the ravine through his binoculars and found no sign of either Tomás or the enemy moving in his direction.

He couldn't sit on this hill for ever, but for the moment at least he seemed to be safe.

The minutes went by, slowly eroding what Razor's instinct told him was already a forlorn hope. The birds began singing in the pines around him, and light filtered over the eastern wall of the valley. Pascual Abaj stared back at him with supreme indifference, and not for the first time Razor considered liberating the small bottle of brandy which had been placed before the stone idol as an offering.

He decided it would probably be a bad career move to anger the local deity.

Tourists came up this hill, Tomás had said. Gringo tourists. And what came up had to go down. If he could somehow attach himself to a group, Razor decided, then he should have no trouble entering the town unobserved. Always assuming there wasn't some bastard down there counting the tourists out and counting them in again. Finding the house where Hajrija was being hidden might be more problematic, but he could worry about that when the time came.

After all, what other choices did he have? Surrender? Heading back north with his tail between his legs? A call to International Rescue?

He walked across the brow of the hill to the side furthest from the town, used his hands to dig a hole under a bush for the two Uzis and packs, and then returned to the stone idol, wondering how long he would have to wait. Tomás had told him that it was the market which brought most of the tourist buses, and the market was only held on Thursdays and Sundays. Today was Monday, which didn't bode well.

A few minutes later he saw an Indian girl toiling up the path towards him. She was surprised to find him at the top, but lost no time in trying to sell him some of the potential idol-offerings she was carrying. Buoyed up by her presence – she obviously expected tourists that day – he bought a bunch of flowers and laid them out in front of Pascual Abaj.

An hour went by, and another. She cast the occasional curious look in his direction, but generally seemed content to whittle away at a piece of wood, and Razor began to think she had climbed the hill more in hope than expectation. He was starting to consider brazenly entering the town on his own when three women and two men appeared on the path below.

As their conversation became audible it became apparent that at least some of the party were English. This raised other questions in Razor's mind. Should he give them a message for the embassy? And if so, what should it say?

No, he decided. It was too complicated, and if they were to look like innocent tourists then they had to be innocent tourists. If he wanted to ring the embassy he could do it himself.

On reaching the summit the fivesome greeted him with nods and then inspected Pascual Abaj, laughing at the gifts of cigarettes and brandy. One of them suggested taking a photograph and selling it to a tobacco company for an advertising hoarding. Razor let them get used to his silent presence and then, while one couple was engaged in bargaining with the Indian girl, he approached the other three and asked if they could recommend a hotel in the town. He had intended to come just for the day, he explained, thinking the famous market would be open seven days a week.

The man, who looked all of nineteen, studied him pityingly, as if no true traveller could have made such a mistake. 'Our hotel is OK,' one of the women told him, 'though the waiters are a bit creepy – they all wear traditional costume.' She walked across to where they could see the town spread out below, and showed him where it was.

Razor asked her about herself and where she was from and where they were all going, and by the time they started back down the hill he was almost one of the family.

'I think there was trouble in the night,' the girl told him.

'We heard what sounded like a gunshot and this morning the square was sealed off.'

It didn't seem to have upset them very much. They stopped to buy and consume Cokes at a shop on the ravine road, while an Indian boy watched from the doorway, anxious to make sure no one escaped with an empty bottle. No soldiers appeared on this road, and none were visible as they entered the town. 'The hotel's down there,' the girl said, pointing out a large, white building with black-shuttered windows about a hundred metres down the street. 'We're going to a café. See you later, maybe,' she added almost wistfully.

Razor reached the hotel without mishap, and went straight to the desk to ask for a room. The receptionist, a plump Ladina with a big smile, asked for his passport.

He reached for his pocket and stopped himself. 'I've left it in the car,' he improvised.

'We have to see it,' she said, her smile still fixed in place.

'I'll get it,' he said, turning away, and found himself staring down the barrel of the gun in Major Romeo Osorio's hand.

Hajrija had spent much of the night awake, waiting for the desperately desired knock on the door, but around four o'clock the old woman had appeared and she had allowed herself to drift off into sleep. The shot had jerked her back to consciousness, and for a moment she thought herself back in Sarajevo, sleeping on the floor of an abandoned high-rise while her partner scoured the buildings on the other side of the Miljacka for signs of a Serb sniper.

The terrible truth had then dawned, and she had braced herself for more distant gunfire. When none came the need to find out what had happened was almost irresistible. She knew it would be a fatal error, endangering not only herself but also her hosts and potential rescuers, but it still cost every shred of her self-discipline not to go rushing out into the night.

What if he's dead? she asked herself over and over. What if he was dead without even knowing he had a daughter?

When the day finally dawned the old woman had gone out in search of information. She came back an hour later looking upset, but still managed a comforting smile for Hajrija. Several minutes of desperate mime failed to clarify what had actually happened, and the next few hours were the longest of Hajrija's life. When Lara finally appeared shortly before eleven she felt as if she had been waiting for days.

Lara also looked upset, but wasted no time in explaining why. 'The news is bad,' she said, 'but not the worst for you. The *compañero* who accompanied your husband is dead. He was surrounded in the market and he took his own life . . .'

'Oh no . . .'

'Your husband was taken by the Army about an hour ago, in a hotel in the town. We think Tomás – the *compañero* – must have left him outside the town, and when Tomás did not come back . . .' She shrugged.

Hajrija felt panic threatening to overwhelm her. 'What can I do?' she said. 'Where have they taken him?'

'Be calm,' Lara said, taking both of Hajrija's hands in her own. 'He is a foreigner, and not just a tourist, and they will think two times before they treat him badly. And while they do this thinking we must tell your government what happens.'

'I understand,' Hajrija said, and took a deep breath. 'I am sorry, I . . . you are right, we must phone the embassy in Guatemala City . . .'

'We try already. The line is busy, and one minute after we try the soldiers appear at the public phone we use. They listen to all calls that leave the town.'

'Then what can we do?'

'I hope you have answer.'

'We cannot call England direct?'

'Yes, but it take half an hour to connect – the soldiers will arrive in two minutes.'

Hajrija ran a hand through her hair, anguish on her face. 'I don't know what . . .' she began, and then an idea struck her. 'How about Chile?' she asked. 'Can you call Chile?'

'Chile?' Lara asked, surprised. 'Yes, but . . .'

'We have a friend in Chile. If you pass him a message, he will call England from there.'

'Does he speak Spanish?'

'Yes, and his wife too. She is Argentinian.'

'You have the number?'

Hajrija experienced a sudden sinking feeling, and then an equally strong surge of relief when she realized that the Dochertys' number was in the small address book she had brought with postcards in mind.

Postcards! she thought, reaching into the travel pouch for the book. 'Just tell him Razor has been . . .' She searched her mind for the English slang which her husband was so fond of. 'Banged up,' she said triumphantly. 'Tell him Razor has been banged up in Chichicastenango. Tell him to call Barney, who will know what to do. And tell him the bird-watcher and Razor's wife are not together.'

'Is this all?' Lara asked, her ballpoint poised.

'Yes, yes, I think so,' Hajrija said. She wondered how 'banged up' would translate into Spanish, and whether Docherty would be able to translate it back again. She thought about the man or woman who would be chosen to make the call, and how they would wait to be connected, listening all the while for the sound of soldiers' boots. And she thought about the man who had already died for them that day.

In his office in the Palacio Nacional, Colonel Serrano listened to Major Osorio's report and blew smoke at the ceiling, a satisfied smile on his face.

'Do you want him brought to you?' Osorio asked.

'No,' Serrano said instinctively. He wanted at least a modicum of distance between the Englishman and his embassy, not to mention the foreign press.

'So where?' Osorio asked.

'Let me think about it,' Serrano said. 'Wait there, and I'll talk to you in a few minutes.'

He placed the receiver face up on the desk and walked across to the window. Another bunch of tourists were being shepherded around the courtyard below, camcorders whirring.

Before taking a decision on where to take the Englishman, Serrano realized, he needed to take another – on what they were going to do with him. No doubt the Kaibiles had first claim – the man had murdered their colonel, after all. But the man had been arrested in a hotel lobby, in front of both local and foreign witnesses, and if the Kaibiles decided to dismember him piece by piece then there would be repercussions. Manageable ones, no doubt, but repercussions all the same.

And Wilkinson might have other uses than the simple indulgence of a few men's pleasures. A military trial and execution could offer dramatic and much-needed proof of the regime's commitment to the rule of law.

Serrano smiled to himself at the elegance of the thought, but decided that for the moment he would keep his options open. The first priority was to discover the whereabouts of the other two fugitives, the soldier Martinson and the wife.

He walked back to the desk and picked up the phone. 'Osorio? Take him to the San Pedro facility for questioning. Use Goicouria. We need to know where his partner is, and his wife.'

He listened for a moment.

'You may. But don't leave any physical evidence. No burns or amputations. This may be one body we will need to put on public display.'

In the third-floor apartment in Santiago de Chile, Jamie Docherty put down the phone, a bemused expression on his face.

'Who was it, Daddy?' eight-year-old Marie asked him.

'I've no idea,' he said absent-mindedly, his mind busy going back over what the woman had said. She had spoken Spanish, but Docherty had received the definite impression that it was not her first language.

'Was it a man or a woman?' Marie asked.

'A woman. Let me think for a moment, sweetheart.'

Docherty borrowed one of the coloured pencils his daughter had been using and, feeling like he was taking an SAS memory test, wrote down everything he could remember on a spare sheet of paper. It all made sense except the one phrase, which suggested Razor had been lifted into the air by an explosion.

Docherty wished Isabel was there, rather than away on business in Buenos Aires. He stared out of the window at the snowcapped Andes, as if he could see through them to where she was.

He read through the message again, and noticed how little had actually been spelt out. The 'bird-watcher' was probably Chris Martinson, the 'wife' presumably Hajrija, 'Barney' the Regimental CO in Hereford. *Detonación levantado*, he thought. An up bang. Bang up. Banged up. Razor had been arrested.

In Guatemala that was not good news. Docherty went through to the other room, rummaged through the desk for his British address book, and cast a despairing glance at his day's work on the computer screen. Maybe he should use this call to tell Barney Davies he was writing his memoirs, he thought. And maybe not.

As he waited for the international operator to make the connection he wondered what the hell Razor and Chris were doing in Guatemala. If Hajrija was there as well it could hardly be on SAS business. He remembered the couple of weeks he and Razor had spent there in 1980, and grimaced. He had not enjoyed dealing with the Guatemalan military, which seemed officered by men with brains, education, culture – and all the moral sense of sharks. The only enjoyable part of the business had been his talks with the leader of the guerrillas, who had gone under the name El Espíritu. That old man had known a thing or too about the military arts, and the other arts as well. And he had been a damned good chess player.

The phone was ringing in Barney Davies's cottage, and

Docherty felt a surge of pleasure at the prospect of talking to his old CO, whatever the circumstances.

A woman answered, and seemed to sigh with resignation when he asked to speak to Lieutenant-Colonel Davies. The CO didn't sound much more welcoming, or at least not until he realized who was calling him.

Docherty told him about the phone message from Guatemala, and offered his translation.

Davies listened, and uttered a short commentary when the Scot was finished: 'Christ almighty, what a fucking mess!'

'I expect you've got people to call,' Docherty said, 'but when you've got a minute it would be nice to know what this is all about.'

'Give me your number,' Davies said, 'I'll call you back later tonight.'

Docherty did so, feeling, not for the first time, an absurd longing for the life he had been glad to leave behind.

Martin Clarke was sipping a between-acts drink at Sadler's Wells, wondering whether to plead extra work and send his wife home in a taxi at the end of the opera, when an employee materialized between them and informed the junior minister he was urgently required on the phone.

Clarke made a helpless gesture to his wife and followed the man downstairs, hoping to God that whatever the problem was it would save him from another hour of ludicrous plotting and overweight warbling. He was shown into the manager's office, where an open phone was waiting on the desk.

'Martin Clarke,' he told the unknown caller.

'Lieutenant-Colonel Davies,' a familiar voice replied. 'Sergeant Wilkinson has been captured,' he said without preamble, 'and I assume you'll want to get your people in Guatemala City on the job right away. If the Guatemalans think we don't know he's been taken . . .'

'How *do* you know?'

Davies explained about the message which had been received via Chile.

'Sounds like some stupid stunt MI6 would pull,' Clarke commented. 'Why didn't whoever it was just ring the embassy?'

'Christ only knows. Does it matter?'

'I suppose not,' Clarke admitted, though he felt far from sympathetic. Shooting a Guatemalan colonel had obviously not been enough for Wilkinson – he had managed to get himself caught into the bargain. The media would have a bloody field day. 'I trust that this business will remain under wraps,' he said.

'If you get your people in Guatemala City moving then maybe it will,' Davies said. 'But if my lad gets tortured or killed because somebody fucks up at your end then I've no doubt the story will be leaked to every newspaper in Fleet Street.'

Clarke managed to keep his temper. 'I don't respond well to threats, Lieutenant-Colonel,' he said coldly. 'And I'm every bit as concerned over Sergeant Wilkinson's well-being as you are,' he added, realizing in the process that it was probably true. If the Guatemalans did torture or kill Wilkinson the Opposition in the House would be queuing up to ask the man who had sent him embarrassing questions.

'I will get back to you in an hour or so,' he told Davies, pressed the disconnecting bar, and punched out another number.

'Get hold of our embassy in Guatemala City,' he told the man on the Foreign Office night duty desk. 'Get them to start pushing the locals about one of our nationals they arrested today in a place called Chichicastenango – no, I don't know how to spell it. His name's Wilkinson . . . yes, the soldier they wanted help from. Then get hold of their embassy here and make the usual requests – treatment according to the law, full access, et cetera et cetera. Firm but not aggressive. And don't talk down to the bastards – they resent it even more than the Arabs . . . Yes, I'm on my way in now.'

That at least solved the problem of his wife, he realized, as the limousine accelerated down Rosebery Avenue in the direction of Holborn. He wondered whether his research assistant would be available for overtime on a Saturday night.

At the Foreign Office he discovered that they had not yet been able to reach the British Embassy in Guatemala City, and that the Guatemalan Ambassador to the Court of St James's was still being sought among the casinos of Mayfair. 'Start trying the other EEC embassies,' Clarke ordered. 'It's about time we found a use for the wretched Europeans.'

When Razor was bundled into the helicopter he more than half expected that the destination would be Guatemala City, where G-2 was probably already furnishing a suite for him in Inquisition-style décor. Contrary to this expectation, the Huey flew south-west for about ten minutes across the jumbled mountains, skirted the western end of a large volcano-surrounded lake, and came down to land in a wide valley flanked with pine forest. Razor briefly noted the approach road winding back in the direction of the lake, walls topped with the familiar glint of his namesake's wire, and several low barracks buildings. There was only one vehicle in sight, and only a few human figures, uniformed or otherwise. It wasn't a military camp, he realized, and, despite the guard towers, it didn't feel like a prison in the usual sense. But it seemed like a very private place, which didn't seem like very good news.

Look on the bright side, he told himself, as they bundled him out of the helicopter. They had fastened his wrists behind his back with wire, but other than that, and much to his surprise, no one had laid a hand on him.

His escort took him down a paved pathway between cinder-block offices, into a one-storey building, and down a long corridor, their boots echoing on the tiled floor. Doors stood open on empty rooms – the place seemed half-abandoned.

One of the guards yanked on his bound wrists, turning him left and propelling him into one of the rooms. The door slammed shut behind him.

As hotels went he wouldn't have given it many stars. Walls and floor were both bare, provided no account was taken of the ominous-looking stains. The only furniture was a plastic bucket, which sat proudly in the river of sunlight streaming in through the single, barred window.

He sat down in the shade, feeling the gravity of his predicament. And not only his – where the hell was Hajrija, and how would she get out of this God-forsaken country now?

He should never have gone down to the town, he told himself. He should never have shot the fucking colonel. He should have argued with the bastard, threatened to expose him.

Cabrera would have killed them both.

Get a grip, he murmured to himself. Good or bad, it was done. He had to concentrate on what lay ahead, had to prepare himself. It might be presumptuous on his part, but he was expecting to be interrogated before he was shot, or whatever it was that they did to colonel-killers in Guatemala. Give them medals was what they ought to do.

He supposed the seriousness of his interrogation would depend on how much his interrogators cared about outside opinion, always assuming they didn't intend disguising the results of their work in something like a car accident. His arrest had been witnessed by several tourists, which might be some help. The problem was, he had a distinct feeling the bastards really were past caring what the world thought. Everyone said they were sadistic psychos, so what did they have to lose by behaving that way?

Razor had to admit he felt scared. It was natural enough. The trick was not to let the fear take you over. He took his mind back to the interrogation which had been part of the selection procedure when he first joined the SAS: those bastards from the Training Wing screaming at him, while their mates beat the hell out of an old mattress in the next room and tried for an Oscar in groans and whimpers. And he had been scared all right, though not scared enough to crack.

In the Gulf War some captured members of the Regiment had gone through the real thing, and most of them had managed to hold out. Razor suddenly remembered the 'fear litany' from *Dune*, one of his favourite books as a teenager. He couldn't recall the actual words, though, or at least only the one line: 'fear is the mind-killer'. He focused on that sentiment until he felt calmer.

Footsteps sounded in the corridor outside, and then the sound of a key in the lock. Osorio appeared in the doorway, and there was another man looking over his shoulder, slender, slightly effeminate, with intelligent eyes. Empty, intelligent eyes.

'Not quite up to English standards,' Osorio said with a smile, looking round. 'This is Lieutenant Goicouria,' he added, introducing the other man. 'He is an interrogator.'

'Nobody's perfect.'

The interrogator didn't seem to have a sense of humour.

Razor stifled an imaginary yawn. The first SAS advice when it came to resisting interrogation was to pretend you were more tired than you were. Interrogators hated interrogatees who slipped prematurely into unconsciousness.

'We have some questions for you,' Osorio said.

Razor said nothing.

'Where is your partner Martinson?' Osorio asked, leaning back against the door jamb and lighting a cigarette. Goicouria simply stared – he was apparently not the sort of interrogator who asked questions.

'I hope he is in Mexico by now.'

'By which route was he travelling?'

'I've no idea. The guerrillas were taking him.'

'And your wife?'

'What about my wife? Do you know where she is?'

'No, but we think you do. You were supposed to meet her in Chichicastenango. Is that not correct?'

'I was supposed to meet a guerrilla who would take me to her.'

'His name?'

'I do not know.'

'Where were you to meet?'

'In the hotel, but I met you instead.'

Osorio looked at him with amusement. 'You are lying,' he said with quiet satisfaction. 'Your friend tells a very different story.'

'Which friend is that?'

'The friend who accompanied you on your journey to Chichicastenango – the Indian we captured in the square at five this morning. He says your wife is in the town and you know where. Is he lying? If so we will have to try more persuasive forms of questioning.'

So Tomás was definitely dead, Razor thought. Osorio didn't even have a name for the man he had killed.

'He is lying,' Razor said. 'Indian speak with forked tongue,' he added poetically, and yawned again.

'Have you heard of the *capucha*?' Goicouria asked. It was the first time he had spoken, and his voice had a slightly rasping quality to it, like velvet dragged across sandpaper.

'Type of coffee, is it?'

Osorio dropped the cigarette and carefully ground it out with his polished boot. He then opened the door and called in the two guards who were waiting outside. They pulled Razor unceremoniously to his feet and hustled him out of the door.

Less than a minute later they were in another room, windowless but twice as large, and with rather more in the way of furniture. There were several upright chairs, one of which was embedded in the bare concrete floor. This one had straps, giving it a superficial resemblance to an electric chair, but the back was open and there were no wires in sight. What looked like a collapsible picnic table stood against one wall, but it seemed lamentably devoid of the ham sandwiches, crisps and jellies Razor remembered from childhood excursions to Epping Forest. In fact, one of the objects on the table looked like a giant condom, and Razor suddenly remembered where he had heard the word *capucha*.

They sat him in the anchored chair, and as one of the guards tied his ankles together the other tightened the strap around his waist. A few feet away Goicouria was waiting, the latex hood in his hands, holding it almost lovingly. When the guard was finished with the strap he was told to fetch a bucket of cold water.

Razor waited, steeling himself for what was to come.

The guard returned all too quickly with the water.

'This is just a demonstration,' Goicouria said, stepping forward to force the *capucha* down over Razor's head. He then tightened the string around the hood's neck, cutting off any access to the outside air, and smashed a fist into Razor's back, forcing him to gulp for whatever air was still inside. The SAS man felt panic rising, and tried to tell himself that they didn't want him dead.

It was getting harder and harder to breathe, almost impossible, and his lungs seemed to be tearing themselves apart in the effort to find air. As his chest seemed bound to explode with the pressure he felt his consciousness begin to waver, the pain to recede, and then the hood was pulled from his head, water splashed in his face, and the pain was back, redoubled in intensity as his lungs clawed for the suddenly available oxygen.

They let him savour the pain for a minute, before Goicouria asked him in a whisper: 'Where is your wife?'

'I don't know,' was Razor's answering rasp.

The hood went on again, and again. Four times in all, before the man appeared in the doorway with the message for Osorio which stopped them.

They half carried him back to the now darkened room, and left him lying on the floor, free to wonder whether he would ever breathe properly again.

Chris and Emelia set out for the south soon after dusk, following the same path which Razor and Tomás had taken only seventy-two hours before. When the confirmation of her brother's death had reached the base camp earlier that day Emelia had insisted on making the journey, and a doubtful Old Man had finally agreed to let her go. She was the only Tzutujil-speaker in the camp, and she knew the way. If the Englishman insisted on following his now arrested partner, then there was no one better to guide him. The Old Man only hoped she wasn't mad enough with grief to throw her life away.

So did Chris, as much for her sake as his own. He saw the grim set of her mouth, the coldness of eyes that had always seemed so full of warmth, and felt like weeping himself, for her, for her brother, for the whole damn country.

He wasn't at all sure he was thinking that clearly himself, but for once in his life he didn't much care. She needed him, Hajrija needed him, Razor needed him. It seemed enough.

The practicalities were harder to judge. Hajrija was being smuggled out of Chichicastenango that night, and taken south to a village near Lake Atitlán, where it was hoped they could join her in three nights' time. There was no word yet on Razor's whereabouts, but the guerrillas were looking, and so, presumably, was London. Chris hoped to God someone found him before it was too late.

It was already too late for Tomás, he thought, as he followed Emelia's diminutive figure down the mountain path. There were no birds singing in the night forest, and even if there had been, he didn't think she would have heard them.

In Hereford it was almost midnight, and Barney Davies was beginning to doubt whether Martin Clarke had ever really intended to call him back. Jean's decision to spend the night at her own home had initially relieved him – he could hardly give her his full attention while all this was going on – but two malts later he was beginning to wonder if he should have been a little more obviously upset that their evening together had been spoiled.

He poured a third, and carried it across to the sound system, where he inserted a CD of late-thirties Billie Holiday and pressed the Shuffle button. The band swung into 'I can't believe that you're in love with me', and just as she took up the melody the telephone finally rang.

'Lieutenant-Colonel Davies? Martin Clarke. I haven't got much to tell you, I'm afraid. The Guatemalan Embassy here has been left in no doubt that we expect Wilkinson to be correctly treated, and we finally managed to get through to our embassy in Guatemala City about an hour ago. They passed on the same message to the Guatemalan Government, who have agreed to let someone from the embassy see your man in the morning.'

'That's excellent,' Davies said, feeling more than a little relieved.

'It's a start,' Clarke agreed, 'but don't expect too much. Our people out there don't have much hope of Wilkinson being released in the near future. If at all. Shooting colonels is not a very popular pastime.'

'I'm sure he had his reasons.'

'Doesn't everyone. His may seem less than adequate to the Guatemalan Government.'

'I understand that. But when all's said and done, they were responsible for arranging the whole business. That must count for something, surely?'

'I doubt it,' Clarke said brutally. 'If you asked a plumber in to fix your washing machine, you'd still be a touch irritated if he murdered your wife.'

Davies had to admit there was logic to that. 'So what's next?' he asked.

'We'll see what the Ambassador has to say after he's talked to all the parties concerned. But I have to tell you: we have zero leverage in Guatemala, and the way the Americans are feeling at the moment they would probably volunteer to join the firing squad.'

'It sounds bad.'

'It is. The way things are right now I'd say there's a better than even chance they'll put your man on trial and shoot him. Anyway, I'll let you know the moment there are any fresh developments.'

Davies sighed and replaced the receiver, just as Billie Holiday started in on 'Gloomy Sunday'. He sipped at the whisky, wondering what options, if any, were open to him.

He was breathing almost naturally now, some four hours after the session with the *capucha*. If it hadn't been for the interruption the session might still be going on, always assuming he would have survived this long.

And they said smoking was bad for your lungs! His smile flickered weakly in the dark room, and again he found himself wondering when they would come back for him.

Think about something else, he told himself. Think about a sunny afternoon at White Hart Lane, preferably in late August, when the perennial dream of winning the League was still precariously intact. Or think about making love in that barge on the Brecon Canal, with the sun going down and . . .

No, he didn't want to think about that. Keep it absurd, like this whole fucking situation. Being tortured by the men the Foreign Office sent him to help. Roaming a country where *Lord of the Rings* and *Dune* seemed less like fantasies than the reality did.

Tomás had known what he fighting for. And, so far as Guatemala went, Razor supposed he did too. His mistake had been finding out when he did, when the only choice lay between a dead colonel and a dead village.

Well, he was damned if he going to come here for another holiday, so his Guatemalan political preferences were probably neither here nor there. But what was he fighting for back home? Peace in Northern Ireland? He had no doubts that the Army had once been needed there, but these days peace seemed to be breaking out all on its own. Hong Kong would soon be gone, and there was hardly room to swing a monkey on Gibraltar. Would the Army end up like its Guatemalan counterpart – stranded at home with nowhere else to go, a heavily armed backup for the police, the ultimate muscle for a government which either would not or could not afford fairness?

He had always thought of the British Army as the best in the world – first equal with the Germans, at any rate – but what did that mean exactly? The best at achieving its objectives? That might be true, but how much was it worth if the objectives were chosen by either idiots or bastards?

Docherty had been fond of saying that it was hard for a soldier to be better than his orders. But not in this case, Razor thought, because in this case his orders had been total crap.

12

The sun would soon be rising on her seventeenth day in Guatemala, Hajrija calculated, keeping her eyes on the *compañero* who was walking ahead of her. It felt more like seventeen weeks, or even months.

Still, it felt good to be out in the open again. The four of them had covered something like twenty-five kilometres since darkness fell, most of them along remote trails through seemingly empty mountains. Their one brush with civilization had been crossing the Pan-American Highway, and as they waited above the road for a suitable space in the traffic she had thought the brightly lit trucks seemed like visitors from another planet.

Since scurrying across the strip of tarmac they had been climbing again, and the path was now angling up towards the last watershed of their journey, a silhouetted ridge-line about a hundred metres above them. They hadn't stopped for quite a while: her three male companions seemed to have finally accepted that she needed no more rest than they did – this *gringa*, she would have told them if she spoke their language, had grown up in mountains not unlike their own.

Unfortunately, this place reminded her of her Bosnian home in more ways than that. Over the last few days she had felt the old despair clawing at her heart again, and this time around the anguish which came with seeing how badly humans could treat each other had been sharpened by her fears for the man she loved, the man whose child she was carrying.

Razor had been taken, and she had no idea where. She didn't know if she was walking away from him or towards him. She didn't even know if he was still alive. And there was nothing to do but keep on walking, keep on hoping.

They were close to the ridge-line now, and minutes later Hajrija found herself gazing at the view from the crest: the shining lake sitting in the vast bowl of mountains beneath the shimmering night sky. And despite the weight of her fears she found the sight still stirred her soul. The star-filled heavens and the vast mirror of water seemed so tranquil, so full of benign certainty.

And, somewhat to her surprise, she saw from their faces that the *compañeros* were experiencing similar feelings to her own. Here in the mountains the Mayan Indians still breathed deeply of the natural world, for where else could they find the sustenance they needed for the struggle against the common enemy?

Chris and Emelia dug in for the day on a wooded slope high above the small town of Chinique, and she announced that she was taking the first watch in a tone which did not invite discussion.

In practical terms it had been a successful night – they had made better than the expected speed, and seen no sign of Army patrols, much less encountered any. But Chris was too worried about his companion's state of mind to feel much satisfaction. Emelia had hardly spoken since their departure, and if it hadn't been for his insistence she would hardly have eaten either. He needed to find a way to let her mourn, or else he feared she would throw her life away, either in some defiant act of sacrifice or out of sheer carelessness.

But lying there in the scrape he could think of nothing to say, nothing to offer or do. How could you comfort someone who had lost each member of her family, one after the other, until only she was left? By telling her that they had died for something noble? What possible goal could be worth such sacrifice?

He crawled across to where she was sitting and took her in his arms. For a moment she beat a tattoo of rage on his back, then carried on mutely sobbing for a minute or more, clinging to him.

Then, abruptly, she pulled herself away, rubbed her tear-stained eyes and said: 'You must sleep – we will need all the strength we have.'

He started to protest, but she was adamant. He lay down again, and the singing of the birds as the sky lightened seemed as cruel as anything he had ever heard.

Woken by the key in the door, Razor looked up to see the two guards entering and feared the worst. They dragged him to his feet and led him down the corridor to the outside world, where the barely risen sun was still battling with the chill of the morning air. There was scarcely time to take in the surroundings before another building loomed, another corridor, and another room. Here the guards removed the wire bindings which had secured his wrists for almost twenty-four hours and then left him, all without saying a word.

He explored his new home. This room, though much the

same size as the one he had just left, boasted not only a mattress but also a small adjoining room complete with flush toilet. The former might be ragged and stained, the latter dry and dusty, but it was the thought that counted. Either his prospects were improving or they were trying to soften him up for another session with the *capucha*.

Just the thought of it seemed to make breathing more difficult.

As if on cue, he heard more footsteps in the corridor outside. The key turned, the door opened, and in came breakfast: a small bowl of chilli, a stack of tortillas and an Atlanta Braves mug brimming with brown liquid which looked like coffee but was probably faking. One of the guards even smiled at him before withdrawing.

Razor ate his way through the food, drank the brown liquid, and did a more thorough security check on his prison. Through the small window in the door he could see an armed guard half asleep on an upright chair in the corridor. The door itself was not particularly solid, but Razor could see no way of breaking it down without alerting the guard. He went across to the window, which was protected by bars and an interior grille. In the distance he could see the coils of razor wire glistening with menace on top of the breeze-block wall.

'Breaking out is hard to-oo-oo do,' he sang softly to himself. He thought of Hajrija and switched songs. 'The best part of breaking out is the making out, ooooh!'

The guard's puzzled face appeared at the window in the door. Razor gave him a friendly wave and lay down on the mattress, wondering what was happening in the world outside. Did anyone other than his hosts know where he was?

It was another two hours before he got his answer. He heard the arrival of the helicopter, and spent five minutes wondering whether it augured well or ill before Ben Manley was ushered into his cell.

Razor felt as if a huge weight had been lifted from his shoulders. He let out a deep sigh of relief, and might even have kissed Manley if the man from the embassy hadn't looked so . . . so fucking English. He was even wearing a suit and tie.

'They seem to be treating you all right,' Manley said, looking round for somewhere to sit and finding nothing. 'By their standards, that is.'

Razor suddenly realized why his room had been changed. 'Last night they put a rubber hood over my head and tightened it until I couldn't breathe,' he said deliberately. 'And when I was nearly unconscious they took it off and threw water on my face. Then they started again,' he added, looking Manley straight in the eye.

The embassy man looked away. He didn't want to deal with this, Razor decided. He works in Guatemala and he doesn't want to know.

'Are you all right now?' Manley asked, still examining the walls. 'No ill effects?'

Razor took a deep breath. 'I'm OK.'

'Good, that's good. Needless to say, we'll deliver the strongest protest we can, but the Guatemalans have already promised London that you'll be treated according to accepted international standards. When did this, er, business take place?'

'Yesterday evening.'

'Ah, well, that must have been before London contacted the locals.'

'That's all right then,' Razor said sarcastically. 'How did you know I was here?'

'Your CO in England got a call from an ex-colleague of yours. Name of Docherty. Someone had phoned him from here, said you'd been arrested and that your wife and Martinson were still free.'

Razor felt another surge of relief. 'Do you know where my wife is?' he asked.

'No idea. According to the Guatemalans both of them have disappeared into thin air. But what I need to hear from you,' Manley went on, taking a notebook from his pocket, 'is your version of what happened last Wednesday.'

With a conscious effort Razor pushed his worries over Hajrija to the back of his mind and tried to give an accurate account of the events up to and including his fatal encounter with Cabrera. But accuracy wasn't going to be enough, he realized, as he watched Manley's face. The man from the embassy had not seen the villages above Zavik, or the dead villages of Guatemala. He hadn't lived with the Kaibiles for a week, or heard the tell-tale scream emerge from the Uspantan barracks. He might be one of Her Majesty's men in Guatemala, but he knew next to nothing about the real situation here.

'I see,' Manley said, when Razor had finished. 'But even if the Guatemalans accepted your story – which they don't, of course – they will argue: "But why didn't you file a protest with the colonel? Why didn't you say you would go to his superiors? Why didn't you even threaten him with the gun, rather than simply shoot him?"'

'It wouldn't have worked . . .' Razor began.

'Perhaps, but why didn't you try?'

Razor held on to his temper with difficulty. 'If I had

done anything else – anything – that village would have been destroyed and all the people in it . . .'

'You can't make yourself responsible for every village on the planet . . .'

'And,' Razor continued, 'once they had destroyed the village they would have had to kill me and Chris. We were potential witnesses. Once I'd fingered their guerrilla leader for them, there was nothing else we could offer them but grief.'

Manley sat there, pen thoughtfully poised. 'You can't prove any of that,' he said finally. 'The Guatemalans deny there was ever any intention to destroy the village, and if there wasn't, then what motive could they have for killing you and Martinson? You see what I mean?'

'I don't give a flying fuck what the Guatemalans think. I know what happened.'

Manley sighed with frustration, as if he was dealing with a particularly obtuse child. 'They also claim that you shot down an unarmed helicopter.'

Razor shrugged his acquiescence.

'Was it unarmed?'

'Probably. It was on a recon mission.'

'Then why?'

'Because if the pilot had managed to report our position we would have had armed helicopters to deal with, and probably troop carriers as well.'

Manley made another note. 'Do you have any idea where Martinson is?' he asked.

'Nope.'

Manley sighed again.

'So what happens next?' Razor asked.

'I don't know. We'll try and get you moved to the capital,

where we can keep a better eye on how you're being treated. The locals don't seem to have decided what they want to do with you yet; they may want to put you on trial, or we may be able to buy you out one way or another. Maybe a promise to keep a lid on the whole business will be enough – it's hard to say at this stage. And there's always Martinson to consider . . .'

'And my wife.'

'Technically she's not our problem. But yes,' he added, seeing the look on Razor's face, 'naturally we have to bear her in mind.' Manley put his notebook back in his pocket. 'Is there anybody you want me to contact?' he asked.

Razor thought for a moment. 'Am I likely to be on the *Nine O'Clock News*?

'Not if we can help it.'

'Then no. If it goes public, I'd like my mother to know I'm OK. But there's no point in worrying her until then.'

'Will do. Anything else?'

'Yeah, ask the warden if I can have some toilet paper.'

In England it was almost five o'clock when Martin Clarke called to give Barney Davies a full report of the conversation. The junior minister seemed more cheerful than usual, but Davies could find little reason for optimism in either the facts or the way in which Clarke downplayed the ill-treatment which had already been meted out.

The only welcome news – which was so predictable that it hardly qualified as news – was that Razor had indeed had a good reason for shooting the Guatemalan colonel.

He asked where exactly the SAS man was being held.

There was a hesitation, and the sound of papers being shuffled. 'A place called San Pedro Norte,' Clarke said at last. 'It's a few miles west of Lake Atitlán. Manley thought it looked like a deserted prison.' The sound of a chuckle. 'But don't get any ideas, Lieutenant-Colonel,' Clarke added. 'This government will not be sanctioning any SAS rescue mission.'

'I realize that,' Davies said obligingly. He knew full well that those days were gone. Maggie Thatcher might have been one of the more obnoxious Prime Ministers in British history, but she had at least been willing to take the odd risk. Her successor had all the gambling instincts of a small-town banker.

After putting the phone down he sat and thought for a few moments, watching the mass of dark-grey cloud looming over the distant Black Mountains. More bloody rain.

Clarke's whole tone had been almost self-congratulatory, he thought. As if the difficult part was over. They had been promised that the SAS man would be treated as well as any prisoner in England, and now the game of diplomatic poker could begin.

Davies looked at his watch, struggled with the arithmetic of time zones, and realized that there was only twenty minutes to spare before the time set aside for a possible call from Guatemala to Chile. He picked up the phone and punched out Docherty's number.

The Scot answered himself.

'It's me,' Davies said. 'I've been talking to the Foreign Office and thinking about what we said yesterday and . . . well, I have a bad feeling about this.' He told Docherty about the call from Clarke, text and sub-text.

'So what can you do?' Docherty asked.

'Not a damn thing, as far as I can see. I can create a stink, but the bastards will just hold their noses. Hell, the way the Government behaves these days one more stink will probably not even get noticed.'

'What about Chris?'

'We've no idea where he is. But that's the main reason I've called you. The people who contacted you must have got your number from Chris or Hajrija . . .'

'I don't know Chris that well, and I don't remember ever giving him this number.'

'Well, it must have been Hajrija then. She may be in contact with Chris by now. They're obviously both in with the guerrillas. Maybe they can do something. This is where Razor is being held – got a pencil?'

Docherty wrote down what Davies told him. 'So you want me to pass this on with our best wishes.'

'It's about all we've got to offer. Tell them to tell Chris not to expect any help from outside. There probably won't be anything one man can do, but that'll be up to him to judge . . .'

'And her,' Docherty reminded him. 'I wouldn't underestimate Hajrija when it comes to a fight, not when Razor's life is at stake.'

Hajrija and the four *compañeros* arrived at the guerrilla camp an hour or so before dawn. She felt completely exhausted, but managed a smile when she saw the man she knew as Mariano coming forward to greet them. At least there would be someone she could communicate with.

He even had news. 'The Englishman Chris is coming here. Maybe tomorrow, maybe next day.'

Hajrija supposed this was good news, but it also made her anxious. With his height and spiky fair hair Chris was even more noticeable than her husband, who had been caught.

'Do you know about the call to Chile?' she asked. 'Can you . . . ?'

'It is all arranged,' Mariano said. 'A man in the City will make the call this evening, and if there is a message for you we will receive it by radio.

The thought that she was connected, however tenuously, with the outside world, made Hajrija feel better.

'And now you need sleep,' Mariano was saying.

A few minutes later she was closing her eyes in a hammock strung between trees, and almost immediately sinking into a deep slumber.

Eleven hours later she woke to find the light already beginning to fade. But she felt better rested than she had for several days, and ravenously hungry. After half falling out of the hammock she went in search of Mariano, and found him sitting on a rock overlooking the lake, eating a tasty-looking stew. Seeing the look in her eyes, he told her to stay there and went to get her a plate.

From the direction of the setting sun, she judged that they were halfway up one of the two volcanoes on the south-eastern side of the lake. Panajachel would be the cluster of brightening lights on the far shore, and the town almost directly below her was Santiago Atitlán. She could see the square where she had rested, and remembered staring up at this very volcano.

Mariano came back with a plate of stew. It was mostly vegetable with just a flavouring of chicken, but after ten hours of walking and eleven of sleep almost anything would have tasted wonderful. He watched with a smile as she devoured it all, wiping up the last drops with the last tortilla.

His face grew more serious as he passed on the message from Chile.

Hearing that Razor was alive and not being mistreated, she closed her eyes and let the relief flood through her body.

'He is being held at San Pedro Norte,' Mariano went on. 'It used to be a prison camp, but now, according to your man in Chile, it is almost empty.' He smiled. 'It is strange, yes, that we hear about the prison next door from a man who is four thousand miles away?'

'It is near here?' Hajrija asked excitedly. 'Where?'

He turned towards the lake. 'Over there, behind San Pedro,' he said, indicating the volcano which rose up beyond the inlet, blocking the view to the west. Maybe twenty-five kilometres as the hawk flies, in the hills beyond San Pedro La Laguna.'

She stared out, picturing Razor in his cell. Maybe he was even watching the same sunset. 'Was that the whole message?' she asked.

'No. The man in Chile says not to expect any help from London.'

Hajrija turned her eyes back to the distant view, and for almost a minute she was silent. 'I need to talk to your leader,' she said quietly.

He smiled. 'That will not be difficult. I am the *comandante* of this unit.'

She supposed she should have realized. 'Then I need to talk with you,' she said, gathering her thoughts. 'Your people have already taken many risks for me,' she began, 'and at least one man has died, and I have no right to ask for more. But I must.' She turned to meet Mariano's gaze. 'Can you find out about this place – how many men there are, what the defences are like? And when the other Englishman arrives here, can you give us a guide to take us there?'

Mariano considered. 'It does not seem likely that there will be so few men that you and your friend . . .'

'The message says it is almost empty,' Hajrija interrupted him.

Mariano raised a hand in acknowledgement. 'That is true.' His face cracked in a smile. 'So we will find out exactly how empty. OK?'

With Manley gone Razor's only human contact was with the guards who brought him food and took him for his daily exercise. He spent most of the Tuesday day-dreaming, and on Wednesday decided to sharpen up his act, setting himself a string of mental and physical exercises. The main danger lay in growing complacent – there was no guarantee that the current benign regime would continue, and if things changed he wanted to be as mentally prepared as was humanly possible.

Chris and Emelia continued their southward journey, walking through the nights and, when granted the cover of mist, deep into the grey light of morning. For Chris it was the strangest trip he had ever taken, a matter of birds singing in empty forests and winds whistling across mountain slopes, of strangers who materialized out of the mist to offer news and guidance, of nights both impenetrable and bursting with stars, of the woman he travelled with, who said nothing and seemed like an angel in the process of turning to stone.

On the upper slopes of the Toliman volcano Hajrija helped with the chores, counted the hours until Chris would be joining her, and looked forward to the return of the two *compas* whom Mariano had sent to investigate the prison camp. This guerrilla unit, the *comandante* had told her, was only about twenty strong, and that only at the best of times. The Army's local depredations had thinned the numbers of the working population, and even those who had joined the guerrillas had to spend time helping on the land. This unit could not afford to be particularly aggressive, and its main purpose was to stay in being until such time as a peace agreement was signed. In the meantime its mere existence acted as a deterrent against the Army's more blatant excesses.

Hearing all this, Hajrija wondered at Mariano's willingness to help her, and wondered still more at the welcoming smiles and unfailing kindness which all the people in the camp continued to demonstrate.

In Hereford Barney Davies watched the rain sweep across the parade ground, conducted the routine business of the day, and waited for news of the negotiations that were apparently underway between the respective governments. He had spent periods like this before, worrying about men he had sent into danger in far-off places, but always in the past there had been the possibility of contact by radio. This time he felt the powerlessness of the complete bystander, and he didn't like it one little bit.

It was just before dawn on the Thursday, with the faintest of glimmers in the eastern sky, when Chris and Emelia reached the crest from which Hajrija and her escort had looked out over Atitlán and its guardian volcanoes.

'That is where my village is,' Emelia said, extending an arm towards the far side of the lake. 'It is called Santiago

Atitlán,' she added, and for the first time in three days Chris could hear emotion in her voice. Glancing sideways at her he thought he could detect a loosening in the facial muscles, and even in the way she held herself. It was as if she had needed the sight of home to let herself feel again.

They dug a scrape just below the tree line, and this time she allowed him to take the first watch. Minutes later she was asleep, her face softening with each passing moment, until he imagined that once again he could see the young woman with whom he had listened to the laughing falcon.

Was he falling in love with her? Or did he just feel a mixture of desire and pity? Whatever his feelings, they seemed somehow inappropriate, both too strong for their current predicament and too weak for the world in which she lived.

The morning went by. He watched the wind slowly disperse the halo-like clouds above the volcanoes and begin to ruffle the glassy, blue-green surface of the lake. Boats began to appear, criss-crossing the lake between the villages on its shore, and around ten o'clock a couple of windsurfers appeared, but there were no signs of a military presence.

It was hard to believe this was a country in which 150,000 men, women and children had been killed by the armed forces in a little over fifteen years. Ten thousand a year, or nearly thirty a day. According to Tomás several hundred victims had been dropped alive into the cones of those three smoking volcanoes which rose up behind the distant shore, beyond the brightly coloured sails of the windsurfers.

Once darkness had fallen Chris and Emelia worked their way down to the lake and began making their way across the fields and tree-covered slopes which lined its eastern shores. It took a little under three hours to reach an observation point above the sprawling village of Santiago Atitlán, and another fifteen minutes before they felt completely confident that no unpleasant surprises were waiting for them in the town below.

The narrow streets were much darker than the hillside, but Emelia led the way through the familiar labyrinth without hesitation, and soon she was softly rapping on a chosen door. A smiling face appeared in the crack, and they were drawn in out of the darkness.

Inside there was light, both the warm glow of burning fir cones and the harsher glare of a bare sixty-watt bulb. There was also a host of people: two men, two women, and more moving children than could easily be counted. The adults seemed to all begin talking at once, in that language that Chris had only previously heard spoken between Emelia and her brother. Every now and then someone would turn to look at him, as he stood there feeling far too big for the room.

After a few minutes Emelia turned to him. 'Gaspar will take us to the camp where your friend is,' she said. 'But on the way I must go to Maximon,' she added, as one of the women pressed what looked like a whisky miniature and a packet of cigarettes into her hand. 'You must come too,' she told Chris. 'It will not be many minutes.'

They set off again through the dark and empty streets, with Gaspar in the lead, Emelia behind him, and Chris bringing up the rear, wondering who the hell Maximon was. It took only a couple of minutes for them to reach their new destination – another one-storey house, larger than most, with yellow light seeping out through the curtained windows. Gaspar knocked on the door, and they were ushered into one of the strangest rooms Chris had ever seen.

The walls and ceiling were almost completely covered with various-coloured paper decorations, and to one side a long table supported a coffin which was liberally appointed with winking Christmas lights. Flowers were strewn across floor and coffin, and tin cans loaded with incense were filling the air with sweet-smelling smoke. In the centre of the bare stone floor there stood or sat – it was hard to tell – a wooden effigy swathed in shawls and scarves. It was only about a metre tall, but both the highly polished boots and the wooden face mask beneath the wide-brimmed hat were life-size, giving the overall impression of a child in adult clothing.

'That is Maximon,' Gaspar told Chris, as he shepherded him towards a long bench that ran along one wall. Emelia had taken a throne-like seat opposite the effigy and was talking to one of the two men who had welcomed them. Both were wearing the same traditional costume – a length of woven cloth wound turban-like around the head, ordinary shirt and tunic, and bermuda-length shorts in woven material of a different pattern. By all rights they ought to look ridiculous, Chris thought, but they didn't.

The second of the two men had already lit around twenty of the candles in front of the effigy, and was now scattering orange flower petals among them. Satisfied with the arrangement, he opened the packet of cigarettes Emelia had brought, wedged a cigarette between the effigy's lips, and lit it. To Chris's surprise the cigarette stayed alight – the effigy obviously had an in-built draught which served to simulate inhalation.

'Death flowers,' Gaspar whispered in Spanish, his finger pointing at the scattered marigold petals. 'They are a prayer for the soul of the departed one.'

The cigarette was now removed, and the opened bottle of brandy applied to the wooden lips, a cloth held beneath them to collect the spillage. The first man was now kneeling in front of the effigy, addressing it with great seriousness, as if he was explaining something. He was the go-between, Chris realized. His job was to speak for Emelia, and to elicit Maximon's blessing or understanding or whatever else it was he was offering in return for the smokes and booze.

And it seemed to be working. In the chair behind her interlocutor, Emelia seemed more at peace, as if a vast weight was slowly being lifted from her shoulders and placed aboard those of the cigarette-puffing, brandy-guzzling effigy.

'Maximon understands,' Gaspar whispered beside him. 'He knows that to free the soul of the dead is also to free the soul of the living.'

Chris was still pondering this when the audience came to an end. Everyone smiled and shook hands, and Gaspar led the way out into the street. Chris had one last glimpse of Maximon, the cigarette burning in the wooden lips, before the door closed behind him. As the threesome made their way up the dark street he tried to make sense of what he had just seen, but his mind couldn't seem to pull it all together. It had been like a bizarre therapy session, a trip back in time, a shuffling of cultures, and all at once.

The journey up the volcano, along paths which wound to and fro across the steep, wooded slopes, took about two hours. For much of the way Emelia talked with Gaspar in their native language, and listening to her voice Chris marvelled at the transformation which the visit to

Maximon had produced. It was as if she had been brought back to life.

They passed the outer sentries at around one-thirty in the morning, and reached the camp itself ten minutes later. One of the figures in olive-green uniforms ran towards Chris and threw her arms around him, tears sparkling in her eyes. Her face looked almost as drawn as it had at their first meeting in the Sarajevo hotel, but this time the cause was more likely to be anxiety than malnutrition. 'Is there any news of him?' Chris asked.

'We know where he is,' Hajrija said. 'And it's not far away – only twenty-five kilometres. It's a prison camp. Some of the *compañeros* have been checking it out for us – they're expected back tonight, any time now.' She filled him in on the events of the last few days, and recounted the message that had come from Hereford via Chile. 'We're his only hope,' she said.

Listening to her, reading the fear behind the excitement, Chris offered a silent prayer that the hope was a realistic one.

He introduced her to Emelia, and the two women spontaneously hugged, as if in recognition of the fact that the sacrificial bond between the one's brother and the other's husband had automatically created a bond between them. Chris was introduced to Mariano and the other *compas* who were present, most of whom seemed even younger than the men and women in the Cuchumatanes.

The food was better in this camp, though, presumably because there were farms nearby. They were halfway through a plate of stew when the two *compas* returned from the reconnaissance mission to San Pedro Norte. The young woman, whose name was Elena, unfolded a map she had drawn of the prison camp, and they all gathered round to examined it by the light of Mariano's pencil torch.

'We watched for two days and two nights, and we talked to the people in San Pedro La Laguna,' she began, pointing out the lakeside village on the map. 'There are only about forty men in the camp – ten or twelve prison guards, four or five administrative staff and twenty-five to thirty soldiers. The only prisoner we saw was the Englishman, but the villagers think there may be two or three more of their people being held there.'

She paused for a moment, then went on to describe the camp and its situation. It was surrounded by a wire-topped wall, and there were guard towers with mounted searchlights at each corner, though only two of these were regularly occupied by guards. There was a single gate in the wall, but this was hardly ever used, since nearly all movement of men and supplies was done by helicopter.

'A hundred *compas* would have no trouble in breaking in through the gate,' her male companion interjected, 'but fifteen minutes later the reinforcements would arrive from other bases and there would be no escape. There are trees near the camp, but the hills all around are mostly bare. If more than ten out of a hundred got back to the volcano it would be a miracle.'

The other *compas* began asking questions, and it was some time before Chris managed to get his own in. 'You said the gate was hardly ever used – so when *is* it used?'

Elena smiled. 'Three mornings a week a truck is driven to San Pedro La Laguna with the soldiers' laundry, and it returns late that afternoon,' she answered.

'It might get you in,' Mariano said, 'but how would you get out?'

'A good question,' Chris murmured. 'But there's one obvious answer . . .'

13

The truck seemed to be looking for the deepest ruts in the track as it climbed the fifteen kilometres from the lakeside village to the prison camp. Chris, one wrist and both ankles strapped to the underside of the chassis, thought the journey gave a new meaning to the phrase 'shaken not stirred', and was reminded of the scene in one of the Bond movies in which the hero had been almost pulled apart on a health-spa rack. When the truck finally jolted to a halt at the gate to the compound, the sense of relief was almost strong enough to obliterate his feelings of apprehension.

A few moments later he heard the whirr of electronic gates opening, and the truck started up again. There was a shouted exchange between cab and gatehouse, and a brief glimpse of booted feet as the driver pulled into the compound. Almost immediately the brake was reapplied, and the truck came to a halt.

He was inside.

The cab door opened, the driver's legs swung down to the ground, and walked around to the back of the truck. Chris had seen the man's chubby face when he first arrived in the lakeside village for the prison laundry, and had heard him flirting with Emelia as Hajrija hurriedly tied three of his own limbs to the truck's chassis.

He was unloading the baskets of laundry now, and making more than enough noise to cover the sound of Chris's breathing. A door opened, a new voice spoke, more boots appeared, and hands reached down for one of the large baskets. The four feet moved away out of sight, and when they returned a minute or so later the driver was telling his friend about a new girl in the village. This time Chris heard the tailgate being pushed up, and the sound of bolts going in, before the hands lifted up the remaining basket. The feet receded again, and a door slammed.

The light was definitely fading now. He hung on, listening to the competing songs of a western wood-pewee and a distant radio. The former seemed more musical, but there wasn't much competition – his time in Colombia had been enough to convince him that Latin American pop music was easily the worst the planet had to offer.

He waited another fifteen minutes, until the risk of disabling himself with cramp seemed greater than the danger of being seen, and then began the job of untying himself. First he released the other wrist, shifted the Uzi around to his front, and slowly lowered his head and shoulders on to the gravel beneath. From this position he could see that the gatehouse was unlit and presumably unmanned, but that the bare ground visible through the gate was now illuminated. He couldn't see the top of the guard tower, but assumed that was where the light was coming from. Away to his right there was the line of one-storey buildings which supposedly housed the prison offices, communications centre and officers' quarters. Two of the windows were lit, but he could see no movement inside.

Pulling himself forward as if he was doing sit-ups, Chris slowly untied his ankles, and gently lowered his whole body to the ground. There he lay motionless for several minutes, watching the buildings which had previously been out of sight behind him, and which according to the guerrilla recon team housed the prison guards. He could hear a faint buzz of conversation coming from inside, but none of the visible windows showed any light.

Five metres separated him from the corner of the building and he crawled rapidly across them, knowing that the bulk of the truck would hide him from any watching eyes in the guard tower. Once beside the building, he pulled himself into a crouch, and began slowly making his way around to its rear. From the next corner he could see the camp football pitch stretching away towards the distant wall, and the fixed lights shining out and down from one of the two unoccupied guard towers.

Hearing the familiar sounds of a football match on TV, he noticed a bluish glow emanating from a couple of the back windows. With any luck the guards would be too engrossed to hear or see anything else.

He moved on past these windows, towards the shelter of the two trees which stood between the large water-tower and the corner of the football pitch. He was now close to the perimeter wall, and about thirty metres from the gate and gatehouse. One of the two occupied guard towers loomed beyond the latter.

He settled down to wait. The sentries were relieved on the hour every three hours, and the next change would be at nine o'clock, but it was the one at midnight which they planned to make use of. Chris pictured Mariano and the two women walking up the track from the lake – they would have covered about five kilometres by now, with another twenty to go. He thought about what he would have to do when the time came, and about his partner sitting in a cell no more than a hundred metres away. He thought about Emelia and the future he couldn't see them having.

The hours went by. The sentry in the guard tower stirred only twice, on both occasions standing up to stretch and light a cigarette before sinking back out of sight. Chris wondered if the man would later appreciate how lucky he had been to draw this particular shift.

At nine o'clock the man's replacement emerged from the other side of the guard quarters, walked across the open space between the gate and the prison offices, and wearily pulled himself up the perpendicular ladder which clung to the supporting structure of the tower. A few words of conversation were barely audible, a louder laugh echoed in the night air, and the guard who had been relieved climbed down the ladder and walked away, yawning as he went.

Chris was just settling down to wait another three hours when a muffled scream sounded from deep inside the camp. As if in reply, someone immediately turned up the volume on the TV in the guard quarters.

He crouched there, knowing it hadn't been Razor screaming, though not at all sure how he knew. Even if it had been there was nothing he could have done on his own, not without wrecking their chances of eventually getting his partner out and away.

He thought he heard the scream again, but it was harder to tell with the TV at such a deafening pitch. He found himself hoping that they kept the volume up.

The minutes stretched out, the night stayed clear. Chris watched the Great Bear slide slowly up into the northern sky, and played word games with himself to pass the time. The TV was still loud enough to mask all other sounds, but as far as he could tell there were few to mask. The lights in the admin block had been turned off, and there was no sign of any movement deeper inside the base. Chris could not see the occupied barracks from where he was, but whatever the soldiers were doing, they weren't taking evening strolls.

At half-past eleven he made his move, working his way along the wall in the direction of the gatehouse. The darkness here would probably have been deep enough on its own, but the contrast with the brightly lit area beyond the wall made it doubly so. Chris had no fear of being seen, and not much of being heard until the noise of the TV abruptly vanished, when even his own breathing seemed to echo in the unearthly silence.

The sentry's head appeared above the parapet, and Chris stopped in his tracks, crouching motionless for a minute and more until the man disappeared again. He inched across in front of the gate and worked his way around the outer wall of the gatehouse until he was almost underneath the guard tower, and only a metre or so from the bottom of the ladder.

It was eleven forty-seven. From where he stood he could see the Guatemalan flag fluttering from its pole in front of the office building. He thought about the quetzal holding its olive branch, and decided a frigate-bird would have been a more appropriate national emblem. They had a habit of poking pelicans' eyes out, and of forcibly drowning gulls in order to steal their catch.

It was exactly eleven fifty-eight when he heard a door slam on the other side of the compound yard, and only a few seconds later when the first cries of the jaguar came echoing out of the distant trees. Emelia was good, Chris thought. Even knowing it had to be her, he found himself wondering if a real cat had put in a surprise appearance.

He heard the guard stir in the tower above, heard the footsteps of his replacement coming across the yard, and took the knife from its sheath. He had killed three men in his career, but all with guns. He had been trained to do what he was about to do, but that was all.

The man came nearer. Twenty metres, ten . . . Chris could hear him breathing, hear the chink of something like a key rattling as he walked. And then the silhouetted figure was in front of him, reaching for the ladder, and Chris was stepping forward, one arm snaking out to smother the mouth as it pulled back the head, the other slicing the blade across the open throat just as the jaguar's cry split the silence.

Chris lowered the dead man to the ground, retrieved his cap and put it on. He started up the ladder, almost letting the knife slip from his blood-drenched hand. He heard the man above him murmur '*Es imposible*', and hesitated for a split-second before putting his head through the hole in the floor. This was the most dangerous moment of all – if the man had time to open fire, then they were probably finished.

Emelia made the noise again, this time drawing it out to cover Chris's emergence on to the platform. As they had hoped, the guard was staring out towards the forest, keen to get a glimpse of Guatemala's most endangered species. '*Dónde está . . .* ?' he began to say, only to feel his head jerked back, glimpse the flash of the blade, know the instant in which the warmth of his life gushed away.

Chris lowered the body into the seat, a collapsible aluminium beach chair with striped plastic upholstery, and fought back the urge to scream. He looked across the camp to the other occupied tower, and saw no indications of alarm. That guard was still sitting in his beach chair. That guard's heart was still pumping blood.

Later, he told himself. If at all.

Three figures in uniform fatigues were running across the sea of light towards the gate. Chris hurried back down the ladder and into the gatehouse, where it didn't take more than a few moments to find the gate controls. He pressed the open button and hoped the hum of the motor wasn't really as loud as it sounded.

Seconds later, with the others all inside, he showed Mariano the controls and pressed the close button. Under the guard tower, Chris gave the *compañero* the guard's cap, and the Guatemalan headed straight up the ladder, whispering '*Buena suerte*' over his shoulder as he went.

The two women were staring at the blood glistening on Chris's hands, arms, face and chest.

'Are you OK?' Hajrija asked. The sight of him had brought it all back. She could almost smell the buildings burning in Sarajevo's old town.

'Yeah,' he replied. He could still feel the blood flooding through his fingers. 'Let's go,' he said.

They advanced across the edge of the yard, and waited a few seconds by the corner of the admin block before slipping on to the darkened veranda. The front doors were unlocked, as they had expected. Inside, a tiled area was separated off from a large office by a long reception counter. Opposite this, doors opened into smaller offices. Directly ahead of them another doorway gave on to a corridor which ran the length of the building. A few metres down, light shone out from under the door of the room they were looking for.

It seemed to be the only light. Chris took a deep breath,

pressed his hand down on the handle, swung the door open and stepped into the room. A soldier was half lying in a chair with his back to the door, his feet up on the radio desk, a comic in his lap. Hearing visitors, he tried to turn his head and take down his feet, but before either action could be completed Chris had rammed the barrel of the Browning into his left ear.

The man's eyes opened wide when he saw the blood all over the gun's owner, and he started pleading, crossing himself frantically as he did so. The sight of the two women seemed to unnerve him even more, and he kept glancing over at them, as if unsure that they were for real.

'Two of your comrades are already dead,' Chris said, raising one bloody hand in proof, 'so we have nothing to lose by killing you. But if you do everything we ask then I give you my word that you'll be OK.'

The man glanced at the two women again, and shuddered. 'Tell me,' he begged, 'what do you want?'

'OK,' Chris said. 'What's the camp commandant's name?'

'Major Toriello, but . . .' He stopped.

'But what?'

'Well, Major Osorio is the ranking officer on base . . .'

Chris smiled. 'OK. I want you to pretend that Major Osorio has just fallen very ill. He has severe pains in the lower abdomen, and it looks like appendicitis. He needs treatment quickly. He needs to be flown to a hospital. Now, who do you call?'

'Divisional headquarters in Chimaltenango. They will send a helicopter for him.'

'And how long will that take to get here?'

'Twenty minutes. Maybe twenty-five. Not much more.'

Chris pulled his sketch map of the base out of his back pocket and spread it out in front of the man. 'Now tell me where we can find the two majors.'

The Guatemalan looked at the map for a few seconds and then pointed a finger at one of the connecting buildings. 'This is where Major Osorio sleeps, but – I don't know – he may still be in the Interrogation Room . . .'

'Which is where?'

The finger pointed.

'And Toriello?'

'The room next to Major Osorio's.'

Chris pulled the Uzi's strap over his head and handed the gun to Hajrija. 'OK?'

She nodded and headed for the door, Emelia close behind her with the Uzi she had taken from the dead sentry.

'Make the call,' Chris told the radio operator as the door closed behind the two women. 'And make it convincing,' he added, perching himself on the edge of the desk, 'unless you really want to die for the sake of a couple of gringos.'

Already he was worrying about Hajrija and Emelia, and wishing once more that one of them had been fluent enough in Spanish to do the job that he was doing.

Hajrija and Emelia set off down the corridor, past a row of apparently empty rooms. The passage turned left, and crossed to another building by means of a covered walkway. Here they heard snoring through a couple of closed doors, including one of the two at the far end of the corridor.

Neither door was locked. The two women co-ordinated their entrances, but only Emelia struck gold, waking Major Toriello by pushing an Uzi barrel into his open mouth. His eyes jerked open, his mouth closed on the cold metal, and he was suddenly very still. 'One sound and I will kill you,' Emelia told him in a whisper, and the look in his eyes said he believed her. 'Now get up,' she said, withdrawing the gun and standing back.

Hajrija appeared in the doorway. 'Osorio's not there,' she said, ignoring the naked Toriello.

'Move,' Emelia told the major, prodding him in the back. They walked back through the silent buildings to the communications room, where they bound the wrists and ankles of both Toriello and the radio operator with lengths of rope they had brought for that purpose. Toriello was also gagged, but the other man was not – they might still need him to talk with the world outside the camp. 'Less than fifteen minutes,' Chris told the two women as they left the office for the second time.

This time they slipped out on to the dark veranda and made their way around the outside of the building to where the lines of barracks stretched away towards the western wall. They walked down the side of the first, and then turned right down the pathless space between the barrack ends, their boots rustling in the dry grass. At the end of the row they stopped and examined the long, low building which stood between them and the helipad. After his morning exercise the previous day, Razor had been returned to this building.

The windows in the end doors showed a dim light.

The two women walked quickly across the space, and Hajrija put a careful eye to the dirty window. Another bare corridor stretched into the distance, regularly spaced doors on either side. About ten metres down, a uniformed guard sat on an upright chair, a sub-machine-gun in his lap. He looked at least half asleep, but Hajrija didn't fancy finding out that he wasn't. One burst of automatic fire and the chances of their getting away would take a nosedive.

It suddenly occurred to her that the man was probably sitting opposite Razor's cell. She took another look through the window and counted five doors, then, gesturing Emelia to follow, edged around the corner of the building and started counting windows. The fifth one along had recently received new steel bars.

She put her hand through them and tapped lightly on the wire grille. Seconds later a familiar face loomed through the mesh, and the feeling of joy almost took her breath away.

Later, she told herself, later. First they had to get him out of there, and to do that they needed to distract the guard. She searched through her English vocabulary for the right words and came up empty. 'Make noise,' she mouthed silently, and when Razor looked bemused, waved both hands in the air and mimed someone shouting. He grinned back at her, raised a thumb in acknowledgement, and then a single finger.

She started counting seconds, and turned to find Emelia smiling at her performance.

They crept back to the doors, feeling hyper-aware of the barracks only thirty metres away, and the more than twenty soldiers who were, hopefully, sleeping in them. Hajrija's mental count had reached fifty-four when they heard Razor rattling his door and calling out to the guard. Seeing the guard get up, she gently pulled the door open, praying that a sudden draught would not give them away.

It didn't. She crept forward, knowing that Emelia was taking aim behind her. If the worst came to the worst there would only be one shot . . .

She was still five metres away when the man suddenly

jerked his head around, and the hand that had been leaning against the wall seemed to twitch towards the sub-machine-gun hanging from his shoulder. Emelia didn't know how she held her finger steady on the trigger, but she did, and Hajrija quickly stepped forward to cover the guard with the Uzi. He looked more stunned than frightened, which she supposed was fair enough. The Guatemalan Army probably didn't get many visits from all-woman guerrilla units.

Emelia moved up to relieve the man of his weapon.

'Open the door,' Hajrija told him.

He obliged, and she pushed him past her grinning husband and into the cell, taking one of the lengths of cloth from her pocket as she did so. 'For gagging him,' she told Razor.

While he did the honours she quickly filled him in on what was supposed to be happening next. 'Osorio is still our best bet for an easy exit,' she said, repeating word for word what Chris had told her. 'Do you know where the Interrogation Room is?'

'Unfortunately yes,' Razor said, putting an arm round her neck and pulling her gently towards him. The smell of her hair was just as he remembered it, and the feel of her lips on his. 'I missed you,' he said, pulling away with a smile and picking up the guard's gun.

The man looked beseechingly up at him.

'Keep nice and quiet and you may live through the night,' Razor told him reassuringly. 'Let's go,' he told the others.

He had done this trip several times now, though since that first occasion they had done him no physical harm. But over the days he had heard the distant screams, seen the fresh stains on the floor, imagined the rest.

Now, approaching the closed door, he heard a soft

moaning noise, and felt the hairs on the back of his hands rising up in protest. It was the sound of someone enduring things that no human being, no living creature, should ever have to endure.

As he stood outside the door he could hear the velvet sneer of Osorio's voice.

He used hand signals to indicate that he would open the door and move quickly to the right. Hajrija should follow him in and move swiftly to the left, leaving Emelia covering the room from the doorway. The two women nodded, and Razor yanked down on the handle, pushed it wide and strode into the room, his eyes taking in the scene, his hands bringing the sub-machine-gun to bear on its prime target.

Romeo Osorio was straddling an upright chair, arms crossed on its high back, smoking a cigarette. His penis was hanging out of his trousers, a drop of semen clinging to its end. On the floor in front of him a naked man was curled up like a foetus, the *capucha* hood loose over his head. As Osorio's head turned to investigate the intrusion his expression went from rage to fear in the blink of an eye.

Lieutenant Goicouria was crouching down on the other side of his victim, his forearms bathed in blood, a thin and bloody blade in his right hand. In his eyes there seemed to be nothing, not even pleasure.

On the table by the wall three fingers had been stood in a row, like trophies. None of them had nails.

There were no other guards, and the only weapon in sight were Osorio's holstered pistol and Goicouria's knife. The twosome had merely been amusing themselves.

For the second time in his life Razor felt an almost overwhelming desire to kill, and Osorio seemed to sense it, flinching at the slight movement of the SAS man's finger on the Uzi's trigger.

'Drop the knife,' Razor said, walking towards Goicouria, and it clattered on to the cement floor.

'The helicopter,' Emelia said from the doorway, and a few moments later everyone else could hear it too.

'You remember how the Nazis used to think of everything,' Razor said brightly. 'Well, so do this bunch.' He nodded towards the stretcher leaning up against one wall. 'Just in case you can't make it back to your cell on your feet.' He yanked the torturer to his feet and almost threw him back against the wall. 'How many other prisoners are there here?'

Goicouria looked at him as if he didn't understand the question.

Razor grabbed the man's right hand, rammed it back against the wall, and drove the blade of the knife through the palm and into the whitewashed plaster. A single high-pitched screech came from the torturer's mouth.

'How many?' Razor asked again, almost hoping the man wouldn't tell him.

'Three. This one and two others. That is all.'

The helicopter seemed to be almost overhead.

The sound of its approach had also reached Chris in the communications room. After gagging the radio operator and dragging him across to the goose-pimpled Toriello, he tied the two men together at the wrist and threw another loop around their necks and a leg of the desk. Turning his attention to the radio, he disabled it as best he could without making too much noise. There were probably others on the base, but there was no point in making life easy for the enemy. '*Adiós*,' he murmured to the four staring eyes, then turned the light out and closed the door behind him.

The drone of the Huey was much louder now, and as Chris emerged from the building he could see it slowly sinking down towards the helipad on the far side of the base. It was another UH-1N, as they had hoped. Enough capacity, enough range, and with any luck it would also be carrying enough fuel.

The guard tower in front of him looked empty, as it was supposed to be – Mariano should have let himself out through the gates at the first sound of the approaching chopper. Chris turned the other way, around the back of the admin block, and broke into a run.

The pilot of the Huey was still a few metres from the tarmac when he saw the two figures emerging from the lighted doorway with a loaded stretcher. It was not going to be an all-nighter, he thought gratefully, and didn't bother to cut the engine on landing. Stepping out to open up the passenger hatch, he found the ugly nose of an Uzi pointing at his stomach.

The army doctor who had accompanied him was receiving a similar greeting on the other side. Both were hustled into the passenger hatch by a young woman in uniform, and after several seconds the penny dropped – these people were not who they were supposed to be.

The stretcher and its apparently unconscious occupant were shoved into the dark space after them, and a male voice told them silence was not only golden – it was also their best chance of surviving the next ten minutes.

* * *

Leaving Hajrija to look after the men in the helicopter, Razor was on his way back to Emelia when the sound of running feet stopped him in his tracks. He stepped into the deeper shadows just as the unmistakable silhouette of his SAS partner jogged around the corner of the building.

Razor blew a single low whistle, and stepped back out of the shadows. The two men shook hands and grinned at each other. Razor led Chris back into the building, explaining the situation as they walked.

'I'll go with Emelia,' Chris said.

They walked back down the corridor to the Interrogation Room, where Emelia was holding a gun on Goicouria as she tried to comfort his latest victim. 'His name is Salvador,' she told them.

Razor took charge of men and Uzi. 'Go and fetch the others,' he told Chris and Emelia.

As they hurried away down the corridor he half dragged the torturer out of the building and across the tarmac, gave him over to Hajrija's loving care, and then went back for Salvador. As he was being carried to the helicopter the tortured man spoke softly and continuously in a language Razor didn't understand.

He gently lowered the man to the floor of the passenger hatch and stood with Hajrija beside the rattling helicopter, her eyes and gun covering the men inside, his looking out across the still oblivious base. He could feel her tension, and could hardly believe how little he was feeling himself. By any objective standards this was a dangerous situation, and yet he felt no sense of danger.

He supposed it was hard to sound a real alarm in a place like this, where screams in the night were part of the aural furniture. Every man on the base would have heard the helicopter – could still hear it – but all of them would be assuming it was someone else's business. G-2's more than likely, and who would want to stick his nose into that?

They would probably have to set off fireworks and start singing 'God Save the Queen' before anyone came to investigate. In places like this people followed orders, and the only man who could give them was lying unconscious in the helicopter behind him.

Still, it was possible to have too much of a good thing. It was probably time to go.

On cue, three figures walked unsteadily out of the distant doorway, Chris and Emelia behind them. Razor turned to the open hatch and ordered the pilot out.

The man sullenly obeyed.

'How much fuel do you have?' Razor asked him, as Chris appeared at his shoulder.

'Almost a full tank.'

'Good. Now my friend here says he knows how to fly one of these, but what he means is he knows how to fly them through a bright blue English sky. Guatemala in the dark may be a little advanced for him, you get me?'

Chris smiled inanely.

'Well, that gives you two choices,' Razor told the pilot. 'One, you can sit in the back with the rest of us and pray, or two, you can fly us where we want to go. Of course, if you choose to be our pilot you'll have to come all the way to Mexico with us, whereas if you opt for economy class we shall have to leave you with the guerrillas.'

The man swallowed once. 'I am your pilot.'

'Then let's go.'

Not much more than a minute later the helicopter was lifting off. As it veered towards the north the only movement in the camp beneath came from the guard in the north-western watch-tower, who seemed to be waving them goodbye.

In the co-pilot's seat Chris was studying the map, and feeling unreasonably disappointed that there was enough fuel for them to reach Mexico. There would be no need to take to the mountains once more, no need of more help from the guerrillas, no reason for he and Emelia to spend any more time together. She and the rescued prisoners would be dropped off at the camp in the Cuchumatanes, along with Osorio and his torturer. They would say goodbye, and that would be that. He would never see her again.

'My brother is in Mexico,' the pilot said suddenly. 'He says Guatemala is fucked.'

'He's probably right,' Chris agreed. But it would also be blessed as long as there were people like her.

In the passenger hatch behind him Razor had securely trussed Osorio and Goicouria, and was now sitting with an arm round his wife, watching Emelia supervise the doctor in his examination of the rescued prisoners. He could not understand a word any of the latter were saying, but there was no mistaking the joy and relief of their liberation.

He felt pretty relieved himself. 'Thanks for coming to pick me up,' he murmured to Hajrija, as if she had just collected him from Hereford station.

She turned to look at him, a smile on her face. 'I didn't want to raise a daughter on my own,' she told him.

Epilogue

Chris parked his Escort by the side of the track, and the three of them clambered out into the mist. The flat crown of the mountain was hidden from view, about four hundred metres above them, a full morning's walk. They started up the path, Chris in the lead, Hajrija behind him, a plastic bag knotted to her belt. Razor brought up the rear.

More than two weeks had passed since their helicopter had touched down on Mexican soil, but in the intervening period all three of them had come to realize that Guatemala was not an easy place to leave behind.

To all outward appearances Chris had settled back into his routine as an SAS instructor, content to see out the weeks which still remained before his official departure from Regiment and Army. He had resumed his helicopter flying lessons and filled out applications for several charity and aid-agency jobs, at least one of which he expected to be offered.

The fact that he found his existence in England flat, safe, almost lifeless, he mostly kept to himself.

Climbing the misty path, he thought about her, as he often did. He wondered what had happened between them, and found that the conventional words seemed even more inadequate than usual. Had he been in love with her? They had known each other only a few days, and yet . . . He smiled at the cliché and yet still felt the power of what it expressed.

He knew he couldn't have stayed, knew she couldn't have left. He accepted it. He had always been good at accepting things, maybe too good. He saw her face frequently in his mind, and every time he heard a bird sing he could see her listening, the way she had that first day in the forest.

Now that the fear of losing Razor had faded, Hajrija's memory was filled with all the people who had helped her – the girl and her family in Panajachel, the old couple and Lara in Chichicastenango, Mariano and the *compas* on the volcano. She had never known such spontaneous friendliness, such a willingness to greet with a smile, such warmth and simple goodness. England had never seemed a friendly place to her, and since their return it had seemed even less so. Now she thought she could detect bitterness behind the coldness, as if the people here sensed that they were missing out on something but didn't quite know what.

She wanted to write something about Guatemala, but what? That being oppressed seemed to be good for the soul? That war was? Was that why she had left Bosnia for England?

As she climbed the path it occurred to her that in previous centuries she could have stumbled on a dead village in these Welsh hills. Not so many centuries had gone by since the English ruling class sent its armies on genocidal rampages through the lands of subservient ethnic groups. But here in 1995 the only bodies they might find would be those of sheep, and the only helicopter gunships looming out of the mist would belong to the army her husband had served for nearly twenty years.

Their baby would grow in peace, in safety. It wouldn't live a life of endless struggle and hardship, wouldn't suffer from malnutrition or have its stomach ripped open by the bayonets of crazed soldiers. All of which was good, and she was grateful for it. But never again would she mistake it for everything.

It was only two months, but already she seemed to be walking differently, Razor thought. Or maybe he was imagining it. He wondered if she should be making this climb, and knew she would only laugh at him if he mentioned it again.

He had a wonderful wife, and he was going to be a father. The rest ought to take care of itself.

But it never did. He wasn't sure if the last month had changed his life, or if it had just set the seal on a process which had been going on for years. His mum had always said that people only understood things when they were ready to. And according to his wife, whose Yugoslav education had included compulsory lessons in Marxist ideology, the old bugger himself had said that problems only become apparent when their solutions become available. Or something like that.

He kept seeing Tomás's questioning face in the dusk, asking him what he was a soldier for.

Barney Davies had been wonderful, but he was only the man who passed the orders down. It was the grey-faced men from the MoD and the Foreign Office and the intelligence services who thought them up. They were the ones who had 'interviewed' him and Chris since their return, the ones who always referred to the guerrillas as 'communists' or 'terrorists', the ones who implied the two of them had gone on a murderous spree, like a couple of armed England supporters lost in the mountains.

By their own lights, they were not unsympathetic. The two SAS men had been simply out of their depth. They had succumbed to stress, to the heat, to their own ignorance – to anything but the call of their consciences.

What did these people know? Absolutely nothing.

So how could he ever trust an order again? He hadn't got a clue.

The mist cleared as they approached the top of the mountain. Just a hill it would have been in Guatemala, but here they could see for miles, south-east to the dark-green expanse of the Forest of Dean, west into the heartlands of Wales. This mountain had once formed part of the border between two estranged cultures, which somehow seemed appropriate.

They took in the panoramic view, not speaking to each other. And then Hajrija untied the knot in the plastic bag, and all three of them reached in a hand. 'For Tomás,' she said, and one by one they cast their handfuls of orange petals to the wind.

Five thousand miles away Emelia awoke, a smile on her face. The poem was lying beneath her chin, where it had fallen in the night. She almost had it memorized now. '*I knew him and still he is there in me . . . I come back to see him, and every day I wait.*'

She sat up and reached for the book which served as her pillow, and replaced the folded piece of paper between the leaves of brightly coloured birds.

OTHER TITLES IN SERIES FROM 22 BOOKS

Available now at newsagents and booksellers or use the order form provided

continued overleaf . . .

SOLDIER W: SAS

SOLDIER OF FORTUNE 1: Valin's Raiders
SOLDIER OF FORTUNE 2: The Korean Contract
SOLDIER OF FORTUNE 3: The Vatican Assignment
SOLDIER OF FORTUNE 4: Operation Nicaragua
SOLDIER OF FORTUNE 5: Action in the Arctic
SOLDIER OF FORTUNE 6: The Khmer Hit
SOLDIER OF FORTUNE 7: Blue on Blue
SOLDIER OF FORTUNE 8: Target the Death-dealer
SOLDIER OF FORTUNE 9: The Berlin Alternative
MERCENARY 10: The Blue-eyed Boy
MERCENARY 11: Oliver's Army

* * *

MARINE A SBS: Terrorism on the North Sea
MARINE B SBS: The Aegean Campaign
MARINE C SBS: The Florida Run
MARINE D SBS: Windswept
MARINE E SBS: The Hong Kong Gambit
MARINE F SBS: Royal Target

* * *

WINGS 1: Typhoon Strike
WINGS 2: The MiG Lover

All at £4.99 net